COULD HAVE BEEN WORSE

# COULD HAVE BEEN WORSE

*True Stories, Embellishments,
and Outright Lies*

*Lynne—
I hope you enjoy these NH stories!
Rebecca Rule
May 2007*

Rebecca Rule

PLAIDSWEDE PUBLISHING
Concord, New Hampshire

ISBN-13: 978-0-9755216-7-0
ISBN-10: 0-9755216-7-5

Library of Congress Control Number: 2006905359

Designed and composed in Adobe Garamond Pro
at Hobblebush Books, Brookline, New Hampshire
(www.hobblebush.com)

Printed in the United States of America

Some of these stories have appeared as they are or in somewhat
different forms in periodicals including: *Alfred Hitchcock Mystery
Magazine* ("Thief"), *Rivendell* ("How the Neighbor Earned
His Nickname"), *New Hampshire College Journal* ("Thin Ice"),
*Out and About* ("Where Selectmen Belong," "A Good Trade,"
"The Well"), *Concord Monitor* ("Mavis Goes to Yoga," "Minna
Runs for Selectman"), *Compass Rose* ("Moosilaukee" and "Jane,
My Ghost"), *Everyday Epiphanies* ("Gram Edie's Tree"), *New
Hampshire Magazine* ("Perley Gets a Dumpsticker"), *Victory Park*
and *The College Letter* (parts of "Dreams End").

Front cover photo by Charter Weeks, of the house he built and
lived in while building another house. Back cover "Dead End"
photo also by Charter Weeks (www.charterweeks.com).

*Published by:*
PLAIDSWEDE PUBLISHING
P. O. Box 269 · Concord, New Hampshire 03302-0269
www.plaidswede.com

*To John,*
*who makes everything possible,*
*including, and especially, the laughter.*

# CONTENTS

*Introduction:*
# COULD HAVE BEEN WORSE

SOME PEOPLE COLLECT stamps or buttons or coins. Some collect guns, dump trucks or culverts. I collect stories and make no bones about it. When somebody tells a good story, I say: "I'm stealing that." And the teller almost always says, "Go ahead." Once a lady said, "Don't steal it; I'm saving it for my memoir." Which was a reasonable request. But most people are happy to have their stories retold, revamped, revived, or used as the kernel for another story. We like our stories to live on. And let's face it, there's an endless supply. Every hour of every day we breathe and walk the earth provides fodder for another one.

Something else, every time a story gets told, it changes. To write a story down is to catch it in one fleeting incarnation. Some of the stories in this book are told stories. (You will recognize them because they're short and italicized.) These told stories evolve with every telling: the fish keeps getting bigger. More than once, someone has told me a true story, I've taken to retelling it, and then, a year or two later, end up retelling it to the original teller, who inevitably says: "You got it all wrong!"

That's what I love about stories: they live, so they change.

The written version is simply a snapshot of a story in motion. I've done my best on these pages to catch the essences.

Here's a family story: Near the homestead in Danbury, New Hampshire—a one-room cottage (two if you count the attached

ix

outhouse)—sits a boulder 20 feet high and 40 feet through if it's an inch. Years ago, when a visitor wondered how such a rock came to be in this place, my Irish grandmother, Elizabeth Moynihan Barker, pleaded ignorance. "I don't know," she said, "t'was here when I arrived."

Whether they're semi-faithful renditions of told stories, or whether they spring almost entirely from my imagination (you'll recognize those; they're the long ones), my stories record the truth, near as I can figure, about people as stubbornly committed to this part of the world as the tree that sprouted from the fissure in my Irish grandmother's mysterious glacial erratic. These stories, too, were here when I arrived. They are like the rocks that rise in the garden every spring—natural, hard to miss, and they just keep coming. I pick them up, pile them, add them to a wall, or arrange them along a path, because they're useful, and because it seems such a shame to leave them lay.

I believe these rocks, I mean stories, reveal a lot about those of us who live here in New Hampshire (or even Maine and Vermont, to stretch the point). We shape this rocky landscape, and it shapes us into Yankees.

Truth is, you don't have to be born here or have any particular ethnic heritage to qualify as a Yankee. Yankee is an attitude.

Example: Over in Walpole, I'm told, four buddies who had retired from far away and exotic places like Massachusetts were doing their civic duty by picking up litter on the side of the road. A stranger pulled up beside them, rolled down the window of his Oldsmobile, and called out: "You boys know how to get to Peterborough?"

There was a long pause. Then the four buddies said, as one, "Yup."

That's Yankee attitude.

Some say Yankees are slow to warm up to people.

Example: One woman told me she'd moved back to New Hampshire after having lived away for many years. She bought a house near the homestead that had belonged to her grandparents, a place she'd often visited as a child. Time passed. The homestead changed hands. *Someday,* she thought, *I'm going to stop by and say hello to those new neighbors and tell them about my family connection to their house.*

Time passed. A sign went up, "Maple Syrup for Sale." *Some day,* she thought, *I'm going to buy some of that maple syrup from trees once tapped by my great-grandfather on my mother's side.*

And she did. One late winter day, she stopped in. Bought a quart of syrup. "How long have you lived here?" she asked.

"Nine years come July," the neighbor said.

"Nine years! I should have stopped in long before this. I'm mortified."

"Don't worry about it," the neighbor said. "We wa'n't waiting for you."

Yankees may not exude friendliness, but we're friendly enough. In context. Example: Family story, told to me by the daughter of a game warden who, years ago, spent a lot of time in the north country. There he was at seven o'clock on a dark, foggy, dismal morning, filling his tank in one of those stark north country towns. Also at the pump was an old guy—"an old salty salt"—the daughter told me, though how salty a person can get in the White Mountains I don't know. He had a beater truck. He was wearing an old baseball cap and smoking a pipe. (This took place before regulations about smoking around gas pumps.)

The warden and the salty salt ignored each other for a while, which is typical. Finally, the warden says out loud: "Where can a fella get a good cup of coffee around here this time of the day?"

The old guy takes a puff. Pulls the pipe out of his mouth and sets in on the roof of the truck. He looks at the sky: dark, foggy, dismal. "Well," he says. "I guess you'll just have to come home with me."

Each section of this book begins with snippets—the aforementioned snapshots of told stories. The snippets are mostly true, and come from lots of different tellers.

Following the snippets are longer stories that have *some* truth to them, deep down—though you may have to dig for it. These are close-to-home stories, arranged loosely by topic, that explore the joys and trials of life in this corner of the universe. You'll find a variety. Some, like "Perley Gets a Dump Sticker" and "How the Neighbor Earned His Nickname," explore the complications of small-town life. Others, like "Evil Earl, Septic Man" and "The Incident on Flutter Street," are cautionary tales. "Bub Goes to a Card Party" and "Jane, My Ghost," are flat out love stories, no kidding. Yankees fall in love just like anybody else. In some, like "Could Have Been Worse" and "The Well," the humor is broad and visual. In others, like "Dreams End" and "Moosilaukee," the natural humor of the characters lightens, I hope, what could be a dark sequence of events.

Whether they make you laugh out loud, smile a little, or grimace as the ice cracks under the weight of the foolish dog, I hope each story reveals something interesting about the peculiar state of being that I call living yankee.

COULD HAVE BEEN WORSE

# POLITICS

*At the meeting of the Municipal Budget Committee, the proposed budget for the school district came under scrutiny. "Right here on page three," the chairman said, "there's a mistake."*

*"What mistake?" asked the school board representative.*

*"Periodic tables," the chairman said, "you've put 'em on the wrong line. They should be listed under furniture."* ❧

*A school board member up north was retiring after having served his district for nearly forty years. A young reporter interviewed him for an article. "In forty years," she said, "you must have seen a lot of changes in the way the schools are run."*

*"Yup," he said, "and I was against every one of them."* ❧

*At Woodford Town Meeting a newcomer challenged the Road Agent's budget, saying: "You overspent last year and I'd like to know why."*

*The Road Agent, leaning into the wall at the back of the gymnasium, sighed. He took the long, slow walk down the center aisle to the microphone at the front, all eyes upon him. Sighed again. Sniffed. Adjusted his pants. Adjusted his suspenders. Adjusted the microphone. The newcomer repeated his request: "We all have to learn to live within our means; what caused you to exceed your budget last winter?"*

*The Road Agent had just one word of explanation: "Snow."*

*Then he sighed, sniffed, adjusted his pants, adjusted his suspenders, and took the long slow walk back to his spot on the wall.* ❧

3

*When the issue of the budget for Sexton came up, as it does every year in the town of Brookline, somebody new to Town Meeting asked, as they do every year: "What's a Sexton?"*

*Grover Farwell stood up, as he does every year. "I'm the Sexton," he said. "And I'm going to bury you."* ❧

*The debate over whether to appropriate $4000 to have the seacoast town sprayed for mosquitos raged on. Finally, Catherine made an impassioned appeal. "Last summer, I tried to have a cookout in my backyard," she said, "and the mosquitos were so thick we couldn't stand it and had to take the party inside. It was terrible. I think you people should stop being so cheap and vote to pay the money to have the town sprayed."*

*Willard waved his hand and was recognized by the Moderator. "Mr. Moderator," he said. "I move we amend the article down from $4000 to $1.95 and buy Catherine a can of bug spray."* ❧

### WHERE SELECTMEN BELONG

*One of the selectmen who may or may not have a drinking problem showed up at the dump kind of unsteady on his feet. Maybe it was mouthwash made his breath so tangy. Maybe he had one of those inner ear infections that upset your balance, could have been. You hear different things.*

*Anyway, this selectman was heaving a kind of a heavy bag into the compactor. Kermit calls it the crusher. When a bunch of bags get piled up, Kermit pulls the lever from inside his little dumpmaster cottage and the steel slabs hydraulic together. Everything gets squished, compacted.*

*This selectman got to swinging that bag like a pendulum, and when he worked up to the big swing to toss it, apparently he forgot to let go. He and the bag both sailed over the railing. Down they went.*

*Luckily the compactor was pretty near full at the time, so there was plenty to break his fall. There he lay. His eyes were open, but he didn't say much. The bags puffed up around him.*

*Luckily Kermit noticed the selectman's predicament. Thinking quick, he hit the shut off. All comes to a halt and the customers gather around, wondering what's the best way to snag that selectman out of there.*

*Pretty soon Kermit emerges from his dumpmaster cottage, looking owly. He marches up to the rail, peers down in, shakes his head: "What the hell do you think you're doing down there," Kermit says. "Get out of there. Selectmen don't belong in the crusher. They belong over in compost."* ❧

# Perley Gets a Dump Sticker: A Harrowing Tale

PERLEY SPENDS THE morning cleaning out the barn—old wood, hay, metal, shingles, tar paper, and what not. Forty years accumulation, give or take. But now it's time to get rid of all that good stuff and make space for his new dump truck. New to him. Like new, just about, since he rescued it from back of Whit Palmer's falling-down woodshed. Since he bored out the valves and lapped them. Since he tuned, carburated, belted, revived, resuscitated and reconstituted it. Since he spray-painted it holly green with black trim. Since he got it inspected and registered. Yes, it has brakes, and a horn, and directionals! Since he transformed that dump truck from scrap heap to beauty. Since he loaded it to the gills with old wood, hay, metal, shingles, tar paper, and what not.

Perley is some proud of his 1935 ton-and-a-half dump truck with a flathead V-8. It's a Ford, of course. The best kind.

Mavis yells down from the house, "You better get going, Perley. Dump closes at noon and it's eleven o'clock now, close to it."

"I'm going." Perley climbs in, starts her up. She's just a humming this morning. It's only about a ten-minute drive to the dump once you get rolling, downhill most of the way. Plenty of time before Kermit closes shop at the stroke of noon.

At the stop sign, Perley has to wait for Route 4 traffic to pass. Joyce, the mail carrier, chugs by in her beat-up Jeep with the flashing yellow light. Right behind her, Tim Ball in the pumper which, from the front looks like a gas truck, but you know it's Tim when you spot his head just clearing the steering wheel, and also from the lettering on the side, "Ball's Septic, Our Business Sucks." Finally, there's room for Perley to make his move onto Route 4, which he does.

Smooth sailing after that, directly into town proper: past the P.O., the 'Piscopal Church, Hildred's House of Hair and Antiques, Mooney's Art Gallery and Gun Shop, Oak Hill Cemetery, the Free Will Baptist Church, Gibby's Gas and Honey-Drip Doughnuts, elementary school, Pine Knoll Cemetery, the Advent Christian Church, Chuck's Tune and Lube, the fire department, ball field, sand pit. Seems like no time before Perley is poised for the left turn onto the dump road. He waits for Joe Fairbanks in the woody wagon to turn first. When Joe spots Perley in the holly green 1935 Ford dump truck with the flathead V-8 and black trim, his head swivels about 355 degrees.

Perley follows Joe in past the chain link fence and hand-lettered sign that says, "If in doubt about where to put it, ask attendant."

No question about it, Kermit, if asked, will tell you exactly where to put it.

Perley knows where to put it. He parks beside the metal hamper to make his first deposit. But before he can even get the door open, Kermit's tapping on the window. Perley rolls it down half way.

"You can't dump here, Perley," Kermit says. "You got no dump sticker."

"I got a dump sticker," Perley says. "But it's on my other truck. This is my new dump truck."

"Don't make no difference. Can't dump without a dump sticker properly affixed to the lower left-hand corner of your windshield looking out. I don't see no dump sticker properly affixed to the lower left-hand corner of your windshield looking out, Perley, and until I do you can't dump here."

Kermit is a stickler.

In these small towns, you find a high concentration of sticklers stickling it to their neighbors. Why? Because they can. And, for some reason, they seem to think they should.

"Tell you what, Kermit," Perley says. "I'll just get rid of this load, and next time I come in, guaranteed, there'll be a dump sticker properly affixed in the lower left-hand corner of the windshield looking out."

"Tell you what, Perley," Kermit says. "You get a dump sticker properly affixed in the lower left-hand corner of your windshield looking out, then you can dump."

Perley sighs. Over by the treasure house, he sees that Joe Fairbanks has found a toaster, a pair of hockey skates, and a pink, padded toilet seat—nice and soft, looks brand new. (Wouldn't Mavis love to get her hands on that pink, padded toilet seat, probably brand new.) He pulls out his watch. There's still time to sneak down to town hall, pick up a dump sticker, affix it, and be back to the dump by half-past eleven.

Where the dump road hits Route 4, there's nobody coming from either direction, which is lucky, practically a miracle. So Perley rolls through the stop sign out onto the main road, past the sand pit, the ball field, the fire department, Chuck's Tune and Lube, the Advent Christian Church, Pine Knoll Cemetery, the elementary school, Gibby's Gas and Honey-Drip Doughnuts, the Free Will Baptist Church, Oak Hill Cemetery, Mooney's Art Gallery and Gun Shop, the Catholic Church. He eases into the town hall yard.

Betsy's manning the office. Perley says, "Betsy, I got to have me a dump sticker."

Betsy says, "You've come to the right place, Perley. Now what's the make and year of the vehicle and the license plate." Perley tells her and she writes it out on the paperwork. "All I need now is a look at your paid property tax and go," she says. "I've got to confirm that you're a resident or a property owner in order to issue a dump sticker. Only residents and property owners are entitled to dump stickers."

"But Betsy," Perley says. "You know who I am. You know where I live. You been to my house."

"Don't make no difference. I have to see the receipt. You could have moved for all I know."

"You know I lived there for forty years give or take since Mavis and I been married. Cripes, you talk with Mavis on the phone every other day about Women's Club, Historical Society, Conservation or some such, get her to donate whoopee pies for the bake sale. Who do you think it is answers the phone when you dial up and say, 'Mavis there?' It's me. It's me says, 'Hang on a minute,' and hands the phone over. If I'm in that house answering the phone every time you dial up, don't that show I'm a resident entitled to a dump sticker for my 1935 Ford dump truck with a flathead V-8?"

"I need to see a paid tax receipt," she says. "That's all there is to it."

"I got my driver's license," Perley says. "Library card."

"Don't make no difference."

Betsy is a stickler from way back.

"If you don't have a property tax receipt on you," she says, "you could go next door to the tax collector and she could look you up in the computer and print you out a copy."

"Can't you look me up?" Betsy has a computer sitting right there on her desk.

"No, that's Lila's job. Go see Lila. Get a copy of your property tax marked paid, bring it here to me, and we're in business. Only one problem, Perley. Lila doesn't work on Saturdays. She'll be in Monday though."

The clock on the wall says by the time Perley drives all the way home, locates the tax receipt, drives all the way back to town hall, collects the sticker, affixes it, drives back to the dump—even if he doesn't get held up by Route 4 traffic . . . well, it'll be cutting things close.

"Can I borrow your phone?" he says. "Mavis," he says into the phone, "I need the tax receipt."

"It has to be current," Betsy says. "This year's."

"I don't know where it is," Perley says. "Maybe in Ma's desk. Maybe in the bill drawer. Bring the whole drawer. Run it down here to town hall, would you? Otherwise Betsy won't believe I'm a resident and I can't get a dump sticker and I can't dump this load I spent the whole morning loading. Well, I'll have to unload it and load it again next dump day. No need of it . . . Betsy," he says, "Mavis wants a word with you." He hands the phone to Betsy whose chins stiffen, whose thin lips flatten out. "Don't make no difference," she says into the phone through flat lips.

Both she and Perley realize it'll be a cold day in hell before Mavis bakes whoopee pies for any of Betsy's causes again. Mavis can be a bit of a stickler herself.

Mavis wheels into town hall yard at just about 11:45, hands Betsy the tax receipt.

"Just following procedure," Betsy says.

"I understand," Mavis says.

It is clear to Perley that she does and that between two sticklers is no place for a sensible man to tarry. He grabs his sticker, skips out to the truck, affixes the sticker, looks both ways coming out of town hall onto Route 4, rolls through the stop sign, heading toward the dump, his 1935 Ford dump truck, holly green with black trim and a flathead V-8 loaded to the gills, humming right along, picking up speed past the Catholic Church, Mooney's Art Gallery and Gun Shop, Oak Hill Cemetery, the Free Will Baptist Church, Gibby's Gas and Honey-Drip Doughnuts, the elementary school, Pine Knoll Cemetery, the Advent Christian Church, Chuck's Tune and Lube, the fire department, ball field, and the sand pit. The gate is still open.

He hears a siren and spots blue lights in the rearview mirror, but he's already crossed traffic and is hammering along the dump road toward the gate. He's making plans: hit the metal hamper first, then the scrap pile, shingles in non-burnables, Mavis's ginger brandy bottles in the recycle.

But the cruiser, instead of hurrying on by, follows.

Perley pulls over.

So does the cruiser.

Perley gets out.

Cop gets out.

"What?" Perley says.

"License and registration."

"I got 'em," Perley says.

"You know how fast you were going coming off that hill?"

Perley explains it all out. "The dump closes at noon," he says. "I've got a full load. Spent the whole morning cleaning out the barn to make room for my new dump truck and Kermit wouldn't let me dump without a sticker and Betsy up the town hall wouldn't give me a sticker without a tax receipt and Mavis had a devil of a time locating it, but she did and I got the sticker and affixed it, and hustled on down here before . . . Oh no. Here comes Kermit now. He's going to shut the gate on me, look at him, he's going to shut it right in my face—*You leave that open, Kermit; you got another customer*—look at him, ignoring me. And I'm supposed to help Cousin Ed haul gravel tomorrow, so I'll have to unload the whole business back in the barn where it came from, then load it up again next dump day, and I got a bad back, or I'm apt to have one before I'm through with this operation."

"Don't make no difference," cop says.

"But Fred," Perley says, "You're my brother."

"Don't make no difference."

And Perley can see that it don't, because Fred's a stickler, too. ❧

# *Minutes*

CALL TO ORDER

Our President called the meeting to order with a reminder that refreshments were for after, but Zoe Lang should go right ahead and polish off that slice of zucchini bread since she'd already handled it. The question was raised: Why did we always have refreshments after, why not before and during to tide us over? Meeting first, refreshments to follow, this is how it's always been done. It was noted that if you served refreshments at the start, nobody would stay through 'til the end and the only reason some showed up at all was Millie

Knowles' double-fudge pecan brownies, not naming any names, Joe Braley. Joe said he liked Millie's whoopee pies pretty good, too.

Gracious Alstead asked had everyone seen that disgusting letter-to-the-editor from Clayton Bowe.

Most had. Gracious passed out copies to those who'd missed it so they could be disgusted, too.

Lily Peasley announced her opposition to the Butter Bridge.

SECRETARY'S REPORT

Minutes accepted with one correction. Page 3: In the phrase "Igno-rent son of a (bleep)," an "a" should be substituted for the errant "e" in "ignorent." Zoe Lang said why didn't Your Secretary work on a computer instead of that ancient Smith Corona with the missing key, requiring "l's" to be penciled in after the fact.

Your Secretary explained that said Smith Corona had served her and the Friends well for more than fifteen years, and it never got any viruses, yet. She added that the town hall computer come down with a virus which ate the tax rolls. And wasn't that a headache and a half?

Martha Kitz, deputy town clerk, concurred.

After everybody had time to review the disgusting letter-to-the-editor from Clayton Bowe, Gracious Alstead observed that the trouble between Clayton Bowe and the Library had been escalating for some time and had nothing to do with the issues stated in his letter-to-the-editor. What did he care about the per-foot cost of the tasteful new turquoise carpeting with medium nap and a ten-year warrantee? The man hadn't set foot in the building for seventeen years.

Your Secretary explained how seventeen years ago Clayton Bowe tried to donate several cartons of dirty books to the library. "What kind of dirty books?" Zoe Lang wanted to know. They were the kind, Your Secretary explained, that Clayton Bowe was too bleepin' lazy to load into his car and take to the bleepin' dump. Your Secretary drove six miles out the Old Bowe Road to the Old Bowe Farm on Clayton Bowe's request to pick up said books, which upon seeing them she refused to put into her vehicle because they were filthy-dirty and possibly diseased from being stored about a hundred years in the attic or more likely the cellar.

It is suggested by Zoe Lang that Your Secretary should have laid plastic in the trunk and taken the filthy-dirty books to the dump herself. It is suggested by Your Secretary that such comments are not helpful and Zoe Lang should retain them.

TREASURER'S REPORT

Bea Smart presented the Treasurer's Report, $594.32 on account. Alice Braley said wasn't that the same as last month? Bea said, no. Last month was $585.04. The new figure reflected interest of $8.88 minus a $1.00 inactivity fee on Fairly-Free Checking from North Country National.

Zoe Lang suggested we might do better in a Money Market.

Bea said if Zoe Lang wanted to be Treasurer that was fine with her.

The Treasurer's Report was accepted without further comment.

Reminder: Dues of $3 per annum are payable to Treasurer Bea Smart. Of the thirteen members on the books, so far—not naming any names—only twelve paid up. Alice Braley said, "Oh, for goodness sakes, Bea, name names." Bea named Alice's husband Joe Braley, but Alice said her $3 covered the whole family. Bea must have missed the meeting at which the family membership policy was adopted. It is a great frustration to Your Secretary that not all Friends read their minutes with care, resulting in needless return to issues previously resolved.

The question was raised: If a new member joined late in the year, would the dues be prorated? The President said nobody had ever brought it up before. Your Secretary reminded the President that a policy of prorating had been discussed in the late seventies, but rejected as too complicated.

The question was raised—When was the last time the Friends got a new member?

No one could recall.

Your Secretary offered to go through the archives to find out, but consensus was Don't bother. So she won't.

OLD BUSINESS

Lily Peasley raised the question: "How many bridges do we need especially since bridges freeze first?" She was reminded that this was Friends of the Library, not Roads Committee, and warned about waving her canes too vigorously in close quarters. Vice President Maureen "Mo" Gladstone removed Lily's canes to the alcove for safekeeping.

Gracious Alstead read aloud and with vigor from Clayton Bowe's disgusting letter-to-the-editor. Resolved (but no vote taken): There was no earthly need for all those capital letters and underlinings, not to mention the questionable language regarding Our President's temperament and Joe Braley's parentage. It was uncouth.

Alice Braley said Clayton Bowe wouldn't know couth if it bit him in the bleep; and how did a bleep like him who'd lived in town less than twenty years manage to get himself elected Chairman of the bleepin' Budget Committee?

"That's exactly why," Our President said. "It's all bleeps on the Budget Committee. Except for you, Joe Braley."

Gracious Alstead thinks Clayton Bowe is a repressed Democrat.

Zoe Lang reported that a man from out-of-state went into cardiac arrest while purchasing a raffle ticket at the Spring Fling. The EMTs weren't sure whether it was the ninety-minute wait in the construction zone, the heat, the black flies, or the double-fudge pecan brownies that felled him. For the Fall Fling, we will piggyback on the Athletic Supporters' Annual Bean Hole Bash. Zoe Lang agreed to head the Fall Fling Steering Committee again this year. She enjoys a good fling.

Gracious Alstead observed that Clayton Bowe is not even a native.

Zoe Lang said: "Everybody is a native of somewhere."

NEW BUSINESS

Gracious Alstead recalled that this was not the first time Clayton Bowe had caused trouble in town. He came out against the new pumper truck at Town Meeting in 1984, and hadn't her cousin Franklin's woodworking shop burned to the ground shortly thereafter and mightn't it have been saved by a new pumper truck?

"Burned up almost three hundred whirligig ducks that Franklin was all set to sell at the Woodford Holiday Craft Extravaganza and Bake Sale," Gracious said. "Poor little ducks."

Your Secretary owns one of those whirligig ducks, having purchased it for $5.00 at the Woodford Holiday Craft Extravaganza and Bake Sale the year before the fire. It's real cute and painted to look just like a Merganser.

Joe Braley said it was shocking what Clayton Bowe said about the library and denizens thereof at Budget Committee, the details of which he can't discuss on account of it was a closed executive session, but it was so bad it was all he, Joe Braley, could do to hold back saying something.

"You should have said something, Joe Braley," Alice Braley said. "What do we need to do? Take up a collection and buy you a backbone?"

Gracie Limfiddle said: "We could kill him."

Asked to clarify, she meant Clayton Bowe, not spineless Joe Braley.

"We could throw him off the Butter Bridge." This from Lily Peasley.

Joe Braley said: "What the bleep are you talking about, Lily? What is a Butter Bridge anyway? Whoever heard of a Butter Bridge? Did you miss a dose of your mixed-up-in-the-head pills or what?"

Our President asked were Gracie and Lily prepared to make a motion regarding the disposal of Clayton Bowe.

Joe Braley said, it was all fine and good to make a motion but who were they going to get to carry it out. An action plan was required. He learned this at a Municipal Budget Training Session down to

Concord. An action plan, Joe Braley pointed out, should include both the action (disposing of Clayton Bowe) and who would carry it out ("*not* Joe Braley"). "It seems to me I always get stuck with the heavy lifting," Joe Braley said. "Just because I'm a man."

Alice Braley told Joe Braley to stop his bleep-bleep whining, so he did.

Gracious Alstead suggested that if Joe Braley did agree to do the actual disposing, perhaps a committee could be assembled to do the heavy lifting, since Clayton Bowe is quite a large individual. Vice President Maureen "Mo" Gladstone estimated his weight in excess of three hundred pounds. Gracie Limfiddle called the vote,

But before we could get *to* the vote (isn't it always the way?) Martha Kitz pointed out that it was already nine o'clock. With all this talk of an action plan and a committee and so forth, she suggested, perhaps it would be best to table the item until next meeting. Nobody wanted the meeting to rage on into the wee hours.

The question was raised: Why did we always have to end by nine o'clock?

Our President explained this is how it's always been done.

Your Secretary pointed out that the vote was premature and tabling unnecessary since the motion has neither been formally articulated nor seconded.

Your Secretary also reminded everyone that Joe Braley had done a fine job of disposing of that know-it-all Southerner who moved in and demanded that everything from dump hours to who got to talk at selectmen's meetings be done just the way it was done where he come from.

"Portsmouth, wasn't it?" Gracious Alstead said.

Vice President Maureen "Mo" Gladstone corrected her: "No," she said, "it was Nashua."

"Not a pleasant person, that Southerner," Martha Kitz observed.

"Uncouth," said Alice Braley.

"He was a rude man," Gracie Limfiddle said. "He got what he deserved."

Alice Braley recalled that it was Joe Braley's special vat of hot fudge at the Ice Cream Social that did the trick. All it took was a taste.

Gracie Limfiddle suggested we revive the Ice Cream Social since it always was a good moneymaker and a lot of fun. The children enjoyed it especially. Besides, by now people will have forgot what happened to that know-it-all from Nashua.

Martha Kitz suggested we run the Social in conjunction with the Fall Fling and the Athletic Supporters Annual Bean Hole Bash. Zoe Lang said she'd bring the idea up in committee and, by the way, did anybody else want to be on the Fall Fling Planning Committee?

No volunteers at this time.

Lily Peasley wanted to know where her canes had got to. She seemed to think they'd wandered off. "Has anybody seen my blee-pin' canes?" she said.

Vice President Maureen "Mo" Gladstone retrieved the canes from the alcove.

ADJOURNMENT AND HAPPINESS ANNOUNCEMENTS

A refreshment of lemonade, zucchini bread, whoopee pies and dou-ble-fudge pecan brownies was provided by the Hospitality Com-mittee, Millie Knowles, Chair. (Thanks, Millie.)

A get-well card was circulated for Mrs. Clarabelle Mason laid out with pneumonia but on the mend.

And happy birthday on Tuesday to Lily Peasley's mother, Mad-eline, still living at home doing jigsaw puzzles and tatting book-marks.

Martha Kitz won the door prize for the third month in a row. If Martha wins next month, Vice President Maureen "Mo" Gladstone says there'll have to be an investigation. The door prize was mums donated by Knowles House of Gardening and Antiques. Martha said they'd look real nice on her front porch, and they do.

*Respectfully submitted,*
*Eleanor P. Hedges*
*Your Secretary*

# PHILOSOPHY

*The tourists climbed Mount Monadnock and encountered the Fire War-*
*den who manned the lookout up top. "How many fires do you spot from*
*up here in a year?" a tourist asked.*
    *Yankee reply: "Varies."* ❧

*Fishing off the bridge, the drizzle steady, fog closing in, one fisherman—*
*an out-a-stater—tries to make conversation with an old-timer. "You*
*think it'll ever stop raining?" the out-a-stater says.*
    *Old-timer reply: "Always has before."* ❧

## WELCOME TO NEW HAMPSHIRE

*Years ago, I'm told, there was a toll bridge just as you cross the line from*
*Vermont into New Hampshire. The toll was five cents—that's how long*
*ago it was. When the family returning from a cross-country trip, anx-*
*ious to get home to New Hampshire, pulled onto the bridge late at night*
*they were surprised to see a car with New York plates pulled in ahead*
*of them. More surprised still to see the attendant in his small toll-taker*
*booth pulling out drawers, going through his pockets, reaching around,*
*looking all around . . . for something.*
    *Then he left the booth, went across the road to the house. Disappeared*
*inside. Lights went on room to room. After about ten minutes, the toll*
*taker returned, transacted some business with the man in the car with*
*New York plates, and the traveling family pulled up to the booth.*
    *Curious.*

17

*"What was the deal with that guy?" the dad, who was driving, asked the toll taker.*

*"Nothing much," the toll taker said. "He come rolling up, flashed a hundred dollar bill and said it was all he had. Guess he didn't think I'd bother making change."* ♪

*When the Old Man fell from the side of Cannon Mountain a couple of years back, word traveled fast through Franconia. Martha-Ann called Rhoda. "Rhoda," she said, "I've got bad news. The Old Man fell down."*

*"Well, pick him up," Rhoda said, "and call 911."*

*Meanwhile in New Boston, the wheels of enterprise were turning. Somebody came up with the bright idea that now the Old Man was gone, New Hampshire would need a new state symbol. Why not New Boston's own Frog Rock—a glacial erratic that looks just like a frog.*

*"Well," somebody said. "If Frog Rock becomes the new state symbol, we'll need a new state motto, too. How about: 'Live Free or Croak.'"* ♪

## ABOUT LIKE SPLITTING ROCKS

*An old-timer named Bill, a native, enjoys splitting boulders. And he's good at it. He uses the hammer and chisel method—wedges, half rounds, feathers. To split a stone with a feather—that's really something. Bill can.*

*Pound, pound, pound. You pound long enough, hard enough, steady enough in the right place on any rock—granite, quartz, feldspar, what have you—it'll give eventually. That's Bill's attitude. "I may not be able to out muscle that rock," he says. "And I probably won't outlast it—but I'm pretty sure I can outsmart it."*

*When he has an audience for rock-splitting, which he usually does because it's so interesting, he'll pound, pound, pound, and the people gather around. Just as the rock is about to split, he'll tell them: "Now you're about to see something no one has ever seen before."*

*The rock splits.*

*And there it is—something no one has ever seen before: the inside of the rock, all its secrets revealed.* ❧

# Could Have Been Worse

LATER, ALAN WOULD claim the blowtorch had been Cornelius's suggestion, though Corn insisted he'd had doubts from the start. The problem was, when the temperature dropped, the tar began to glop. Pretty soon it was nothing but daubs and goobers. Corn later claimed to have advised giving it up at that point. Calling it a day.

"It's October," Alan said, "butting up against November. We were lucky to get this one warm day. Might not get another until spring, and then what's Gram going to do?"

The roof on Gert's woodshed had been leaking bad. It hadn't reached the Arethusa Falls stage yet, but it might in the next hard rain. Which was why her step-grandson Alan and the cousins Pod and Cornelius replaced the rotten boards with plywood and the rotten shingles with double-coverage. They were trying to anyway.

And things were going right along smooth, too. For awhile.

The surprise of Indian summer warmed the roof, melted the tar, and heated the boys up so much they had to have a couple few beers to cool down. They ripped up the old shingles and sailed them like flat black frisbees into the bed of Cornelius's pickup. That was fun.

They pried up the old boards, laid in new plywood. Pod spread tar with a trowel. Alan rolled out the double-coverage and trimmed the ends with a utility knife. Then Cornelius come along behind, nailing.

The system was working beautiful until the temperature dropped and the tar seized up. Pod held out the trowel between stiff gloves. "Check this out," he said. The tar didn't drip. Didn't ooze. It defied gravity. It was chunkified—a definite oh-shit.

Oh-shit is the home handyman term for a problem that must be corrected before work can proceed. Like mixing the mortar too watery or too thick. Like failing to level the footer so after ten or twelve layers of brick, the tilt becomes precarious. Like spiking your hand to a beam with a power-nailer.

Cornelius and Alan voted against renting a power-nailer for Gert's roof on account of Pod's attraction to all things mechanical and his tendency to injure himself with them. He could have been a master criminal he had so few fingerprints. Pod didn't do well with power tools. When he fell in love with a chipper-shredder at the Deerfield Fair, his Uncle Perley put it best: "That young Pod gets himself a chipper-shredder and it's just a matter of time before he's squirting out the other end."

Which is why, when it came to Gert's roof, Pod was vice president in charge of spreading tar.

The boys meant well. They did. "Gram," Alan told her, magnanimous over supper, "there's no sense you hiring that job out and paying through the nose. A lot of these contractors, they don't know what they're doing. Don't care. And the ones that do know what they're doing are apt to take advantage of an elderly person."

"Who you calling an old lady?" Gert said.

"You," observed Perley, who was just her same age less two months. The only reason she put up with Perley and his sass, he'd been married to her favorite cousin, Mavis, for forty years, give or take, and she'd gotten used to him.

"What say I get the boys together some weekend, Gram," Alan said, "and we'll all pitch in and have that shed re-roofed before you can say pass the salt. Pass the salt," he added.

Perley passed the salt.

"How's your high blood pressure, Alan," Mavis said.

"Good," Alan said. "Beautiful."

"I bet Perley would help," Gert said. "He enjoys roof work. Why he's been known to set on the roof all afternoon in a blizzard. After the ladder fell."

"Last Christmas, when I arrived home from the Woodford Holiday Craft Extravaganza and Bake Sale, there he was," Mavis said. "Setting up on the roof, covered with snow, contemplating his place in the universe. The decorations looked nice though."

Normally, you'd repair a leaking roof in the summer, preferably August, when the tar stays melty all day and goes down easy as paint. If the boys had found time that next weekend or the one after or the one after that maybe things would have worked out different. But they didn't.

By mid-October, Gert had almost given up hope. Common knowledge: once deer season started all extracurricular activities came to an abrupt halt. Mavis suggested calling Mr. Hedley Pitcher, who did odd jobs. But Gert said, no, she'd give the boys the benefit of the doubt. They'd get the job done sometime, probably.

"When?" Mavis said.

"When they get around to it." Gert's second husband Herman had been the same way. If a job needed doing, Herman had to ponder it, look it over, discuss it thoroughly, and walk all around the possibilities. Of course, once he settled on a plan and set aside some time, chances were he wouldn't have just the right tools or materials on hand. Quite a number of times, when he finally got around to doing a thing, Gert had already done it. Then, of course, he'd comment on the quality of her work. He would have nailed the clapboards on the bottom instead of the top; used regular varnish instead of the fast drying, mixed the wood filler with Elmer's glue to prevent shrinkage. "He had a fit about the odds and ends I used to cover the gaps in the floor of the bathroom closet. I waited as long as I could, Mavis, but the cold air was pouring in and I was afraid the pipes would freeze. Not to mention the rats."

"Nasty things." Mavis said, "Brazen, too. When we had goats, some mornings a rat or two would set right there in the pen, big as life. I'd throw stones, but if I didn't hit them between the eyes or on the top of the head, do you think they'd move? They would not move. They'd set right there. Brazen. Course if a rat had a fluffy tail like a squirrel, you wouldn't mind so much. It's that skinny tail that gets me."

"I don't like any part of 'em," Gert said. "There's nothing at all about a rat that I enjoy." Then she told how she was in the bathroom with her *Reader's Digest* minding her own business when she heard a commotion in the aforementioned closet. Pretty soon a snout poked out between the slatted doors and a head and a pair of little bow legs. "I let that rat know he was not welcome in no uncertain terms. But he just stares at me. 'Who the hell are you and what's your problem, lady?' Then he gets a kind of a pained expression, as if all my whooping and hollering gave him a little rat migraine. I'm doing a tap dance on the toilet rim. Didn't have time to lower the cover."

Mavis said, "When the neighbor was fixing his upstairs and had his house all tore apart, I looked out my kitchen window, true story, and halfway up the ladder leaning against the building, something brown clung to a rung. At first I thought it was a squirrel. It wasn't a squirrel."

"Was it coming or going?" Gert said.

"Just setting there," Mavis said. "Contemplating its place in the universe."

Yes, Cornelius had provided the blowtorch from the tool chest in the back of his truck, but he had not been enthusiastic about using it. Later, he and Alan voted that if the question ever came up as to who had the bright idea of the blowtorch, they'd blame Pod. Pod wouldn't know the difference.

They agreed that there had been a conversation concerning the problem of the chunkified tar. The three of them sat side by side on the staging, legs dangling, watching the sun slide down. Maybe they could wrap the bucket with heating tape. But getting the tar up to temperature that way would take hours. And Cornelius had neglected to bring his heavy-duty extension cord. They didn't have any heating tape either, come to think of it.

"Start up your truck, Corn," Pod said, "and we'll set the bucket on the engine block." But Corn didn't want that bucket anywhere near his engine block and its delicate workings. They could sneak the bucket into the house and set it on a register or close beside the fired-up woodstove, but if Gert caught them, she'd be ugly. She was a picky housekeeper, wouldn't even let them in at noon for a sandwich because they were so grubby and might stick to the furniture.

They had to eat outside on the picnic table. They had to pee in the woods. You got to hand it to Gert though—she joined them. For lunch that is.

"Going right along smooth," Pod announced to Gert and the cosmos during that Al Fresco meal. (Pod thought Al Fresco was some Italian guy who invented picnics.) Which was a dangerous thing to say, almost like bragging, tempting fate so to speak. Discussing their fates afterwards, among themselves, Alan and Cornelius agreed that Pod wouldn't remember who lit the blowtorch and held the blue flame to the bottom of the metal bucket half full of tar. They could hardly recall themselves. And what they did recall, over time, became more and more confusing. Who turned the bucket to the flame when the tar got stubborn, thinking maybe it'd melt quicker from the top than the bottom?

"I thought it was you," Alan said.

"I'm pretty sure it was you," Cornelius said.

"Must have been Pod."

"Not one of my brighter moves," Pod lamented.

It might have been Cornelius who declared the first oh-shit.

Somebody dropped the flaming bucket, that was for sure, startled by the whoosh of ignition.

Somebody tried to stop it rolling with his boot.

Somebody said, "Geesh, don't let the staging catch fire with all those bits and pieces of double-coverage. They'll go up like birch bark."

Somebody said, "Knock that bucket away from the ladder, would you?"

Somebody said, "The ladder won't burn. It's aluminum."

Somebody noticed that the bulk of the conflagration was between them and the ladder anyway, making descent difficult.

Somebody confirmed oh-shit status and tried to snuff the flames by dropping a sheet of plywood. The plywood failed to snuff the flames, which curled out from under the edges, and in fact caught fire itself.

Somebody yelled, "Jump."

Pod didn't actually remember jumping. "But I must have," he said. "How else could I have landed in Aunt Gert's yew?"

Somebody, Gert seemed to think it was Alan, ran into the house, tracking tar and sawdust and soot and dirt; must have been Alan, because she remembered his exact words: "Gram," he said, "the repair to your shed roof is not going along as smooth as we had hoped."

Perley and Mavis, who happened to have their scanner tuned to the emergency channel, wheeled in just about the same time as the fire truck, which is to say, a little late for the main event. Perley stood in the driveway observing the fire fighters as they packed up their large hoses. In the glow, he spotted the shape of his brother, Fred, writing all about it in his police notebook.

Mavis stepped into the house and there sat Gert at the kitchen table. There had been just under two cord of wood, give or take, stored in that shed. "Could have been worse," Mavis said. "Could have been full."

Mavis made coffee.

"Didn't you used to keep your lawn mower in that shed? And your rototiller?"

"I moved them to the barn and the wheelbarrow and garden tools, too," Gert said, "because of the leaky roof."

"That was lucky," Mavis said. "At least it wasn't the barn or, God forbid, the main house the boys were fixing." The shed stood just twenty feet corner to corner from the east ell of the house. "Could have been worse," Mavis said. "Could have been windy."

She and Gert drank coffee. They ate Fig Newtons straight from the package. "When Perk Perkins's trailer blew up from the gas leak, it was mud season. Remember? Remember how the fire trucks got stuck at the bottom of the hill, and the ambulance got stuck too (it was a good thing Perk was blown clear), not to mention the cruiser. They had an awful time extricating those vehicles, as I recall."

"It was a mess," Gert said.

"At least it's not mud season," Mavis said.

Gert blew her nose on a paper towel. She flicked a Fig Newton crumb across the flowered plastic tablecloth like a tiny puck.

"Nobody got hurt, that's the main thing," Mavis said. "The boys are hardly even singed. It certainly could have been worse." Just then Perley burst in the door, smelling of smoke. He sniffed, wiped his feet on the mat, hung his hat and coat on the peg.

"Where are they?" Gert said.

He flicked his head to indicate that the roofers were still outside.

Mavis stepped to the window and pushed aside the curtain. She saw the three of them eerily silhouetted in the strobing red lights of the pumper truck and the strobing blue lights of the cruiser. They sat on top of the picnic table, side by side, like hear-no-evil, see-no-evil, speak-no-evil monkeys.

Pod hung his head. Alan seemed to be studying the buckle of Orion's belt, which had just cleared the smoky horizon. Cornelius couldn't take his eyes off the place where Gert's shed used to be. Maybe if he stared long enough and hard enough it would reappear.

"What are they doing?" Gert said. She didn't get up from the table. Didn't have the heart to look.

"Just sitting there," Mavis said, "quiet; contemplating their place in the universe."

# The Incident on Flutter Street

SO I'M DRIVING up the big hill on Flutter Street taking the shortcut to the village to meet my friend Mo (also a widow) for fish and chips at Harley's Diner. Harley serves a nice fish and chips, not too greasy and no bones. Once I found a bone, but that's not too bad, one bone, considering the amount of the fish and chips I've consumed at Harley's over the years. And the price is reasonable. Mo usually has the fried clams with coleslaw. She loves fried clams and coleslaw. I give her my coleslaw from the fish and chips because it comes with it and I do not enjoy coleslaw. In fact anything made with mayonnaise I find disgusting, but that's another story.

After we eat our lunch at Harley's, we're off to Bingo for one-thirty when the early-bird games start. Sometimes I win, but usually not. I've won fifty dollars quite a few times, a hundred dollars three times, and once I won the five hundred. Mo's record is similar, except she never won the five hundred, but maybe today's her day. You never know with Bingo. You never know when it'll be your lucky day.

So I'm driving along Flutter Street taking the shortcut to the village and I come up behind this little blue Subaru, low to the ground with Massachusetts plates. I'm pretty sure the man is lost, because he slows down at intersections and speeds up on the straight. He barely made the hairpin curve by the cemetery; it snuck up on him. So the whole length of Flutter Street which goes on for miles and miles—it runs all the way from South Woodford to the Village—he's looking around for something. I can see his big head turning this way and that way. He's reading the signs, trying to, on the little roads that branch off from Flutter Street, mostly dead-ends on account of the river on one side and Hosshead Hill on the other. Also, some of the young people, every once in a while, switch those signs around just for the hell of it. A lot of people get lost on Flutter Street. They think they're going somewhere when really they're going somewhere else.

Anyway, I'm driving the length of Flutter Street behind this little blue Subaru, low to the ground with Massachusetts plates, and we come to the big hill. The little blue Subaru revs up in anticipation. The big hill on Flutter Street is a steep climb for a little car. I hang back to let him get a good head start. You never know on a hill.

What I didn't know at the time was what had occurred just a couple of minutes before the little blue Subaru started its ascent. It seems that Maxwell Braley had ascended the hill just ahead of us, his truck loaded heavy with manure and headed for Cinnamon Farm. As my husband George would have said, "He was off to shit the field." That's what they call it. Shitting the field. It's a technical term.

Unfortunately, Maxwell thumped the frost heave at the bottom of the big hill on Flutter Street and unbeknownst to him the tailgate on his truck flopped open, so as he ascended the hill, unbeknownst to him, that substantial load of ripe manure sluiced out the back and created what can only be called a shit slick, about eight feet wide, two feet deep, and who knows how long. Let's just say a substantial portion of the steep part of the big hill on Flutter Street was pretty well buried.

The little blue Subaru, revved to make the hill, didn't hesitate. It plowed right into that huge shit slick. When the wheels started to spin, he must have shifted into four-wheel-drive, because he managed to keep plowing along until he'd plowed right smack into the middle of it. It was then the man in the little blue Subaru, low to the ground with Massachusetts plates, made his big mistake.

He stopped.

My theory is that he didn't realize what he'd gotten into until he was too far into it to turn back. At that point, perhaps, the odor of the well-ripened manure seeped in through the closed windows of the little blue Subaru and all of a sudden it struck him. All of a sudden he smelled what he'd gotten himself into and for some reason—my husband George would have said his brain slipped into neutral—he stopped.

There he sat, halfway up the steep part of the big hill on Flutter Street, buried to the wheel wells in that enormous pungent load. It was not his lucky day.

So I stop several yards back from the trouble spot and I look and at the crest of the hill, I see Maxwell Braley walking slow with a shovel that looked awful small, considering.

Later, I'm telling the story to Mo at Harley's Diner as we enjoy our pudding desserts. She has chocolate but I don't feel like chocolate, so I go for the rice. We've still got a few minutes before the early birds at Bingo. "What did you do, Frances?" Mo says between spoonfuls. "What did Maxwell Braley do? What did the poor lost man from Massachusetts in the little blue Subaru do?"

"I can't tell you what they did, Mo," I say. "I can only tell you what I did. I had someplace to be. I drove around it." ❧

# COMMERCE

*Linwood used to sell picnic tables out front of his place. For sixteen dollars each—that's how long ago it was. Long time ago. A fella pulled up in a big old truck with out-of-state plates; probably summer people. He looked the picnic tables over. "Sixteen dollars," he says.*

*"Yup," Linwood says.*

*"How long does it take you to make one of those picnic tables?"*

*Linwood thought a while. "Oh," he says, "About four hours."*

*"Four hours," Fella says—doing some quick calculations in his head. (He was a smart fella.) "Four hours, sixteen dollars. That's about four dollars an hour, isn't it?"*

*"Yup," Linwood says.*

*Fella says, "Well, could you make me a picnic table for three dollars an hour?"*

*"Sure," Linwood says. "But it would take a little longer."* ❧

FOR SALE (IF YOU CAN LOCATE IT)

*The deed to the property in question read as follows: Starting at the pine tree where you and I stood yesterday . . .* ❧

*In Sandwich, I'm told, years ago, a new fella moves into town to be caretaker for one of the big houses. At the general store he stocks up on supplies—milk, butter, potatoes, baked beans in a can, etc. He also asks for a pack of Lucky Strikes. The storekeeper packs all the stuff into a paper bag, and when the fella gets home he discovers he's got a carton of Lucky Strikes instead of a pack.*

*He checks the slip—sure enough, he only paid for a pack.*

*The next week when he goes into the store, he says to the storekeeper: "You didn't realize it, but last week you gave me a carton of Lucky Strikes, and I only paid for a pack."*

*The storekeeper nods. "Oh," he says solemnly, "I realized it."* ❧

*Morton took a mortgage out on a heifer for $10 from his neighbor, Maxwell, who lived up top the hill.*

*Time passed.*

*One morning Old Maxwell come walking down by Morton's farm and Morton happened to be out front digging out a plugged culvert. Maxwell says: "Morton, you owe me $10 for that mortgage on that white-faced heifer."*

*Morton says: "Ha! I done fooled you. I ate that heifer."*

*Old Maxwell, a dairy farmer with big hands, pinched two huge sausage fingers together and reached into the bib of his overalls. He pulled out a folded paper. "Ha!" he said. "But you didn't eat the mortgage."* ❧

# *The Well*

URBAN SAYS, "THERE'S all kinds of stuff in the ground around my place. Mica, feldspar, quartz, beryl. You better go careful when you're digging. Don't know what you're going to find. Nineteen sixty-two, Mother got it into her head she wanted a well. She was sick of the dug well drying up in hot weather. She wanted an artesian well."

Royal says, "Was she adamant?"

Urban says, "I don't know about that, but her sister had an artesian well, so she had to have one, too. Got it into her head, she just had to have an artesian well and an indoor bathroom with a tub. Had to have it.

"Hired the job out and the fellas come in with their big truck and that big old thumpa-thumpa drill. They commenced to drilling. Course you had to pay by the foot, so the deeper they went, the more it cost you. You could practically see the dollar bills floating up from that hole and out of sight.

"They drilled down about two-hundred feet, just a-grinning, 'til they drilled into a mess of mica.

"Course it was soft and they didn't realize until the whole thing caved in on itself. The thumpa-thumpa got buried. They couldn't extract it, couldn't afford to leave it. Had to bring in the derricks and pulleys and earth movers and so forth to dig out what they lost on the first pass. By God, if they didn't drill right into that pocket of mica again and lose that bunch, too.

"It was some mess I'll tell you. And there was no way Mother and I were going to shell out for that debacle."

Royal says, "Did your mother ever get her artesian, Urban?"

Urban says, "They just kept bringing in more equipment and losing it down the hole—tractors, bulldozers, cranes, bigger cranes. You ever see that ship-moving crane up to Bath Ironworks—well it wa'n't that big, but pretty close. The hole got bigger and bigger. Pretty soon the barn slid in. Pretty soon the house slid in. Mother and I had to sell off the land and move. They used to call that part of town West Woodford."

Royal says, "I heard of North, South, and East Woodford. But no West Woodford. There is no West Woodford, Urban."

Urban says, "Not any more there isn't. It's all down in the hole." ❧

# A Good Trade

"WHAT DO YOU want with a fishing boat anyway, Perley?" Mavis says. "It's not like you fish. You haven't fished in years. And when you did, you didn't catch anything."

"Now that's cruel," Perley says. "Father and Fred and me used to catch a lot of fish, especially during the Mayfly hatch. During the Mayfly hatch you didn't even hardly need a pole, they'd jump right into the boat, practically; so all you had to do, pretty much, was discourage them from jumping back out."

"I guess that was before my time," she says.

Father's boat was a thousand-pound (seemed like) skiff. It took three of them to lift the bow, and then they'd have to run around the other end, seesaw it down the launch. Must have been oak or elm; maybe cast iron. Painted over so many times it was hard to tell. The paint alone must have weighed a hundred pounds, not to mention the hardware.

Loaded with bait, tackle, picnic, and the three of them mummi-fied in life jackets (poor swimmers, even worse floaters), the boat set so low in the water, you had to be careful not to move quick or lean heavy, especially once you started hauling 'em in.

"Whatever happened to Dad's old boat?" Perley asks Fred the next time he sees him.

"Burned it," Fred says. "Dumped me one too many times, and the last time it flipped, landed on my head and concussed me. I figured eventually this bastard's going to drown me. So I chopped it up and tossed it on the bonfire."

"Probably for the best," Perley says, though he feels a little sad about it. Sometimes he feels like an old boat himself, especially when Mavis gives him the "look" and says, "Keep it up. You just keep it up, Perley." Thought crosses his mind that she might chop him up and toss him on the bonfire if he doesn't reform. And he's too old to reform.

Richit's aluminum boat is a fourteen-foot Scowcraft with enough draft so you couldn't tip it if you tap danced on the gunnel. So Richit says.

"I don't enjoy a tippy boat," Perley says.

"This baby sits in the water like a cork in ketchup," Richit says. "My cousin Gob and I tried to tip it over once, just to see. Couldn't do it. And Gob's a big boy."

"It's a fair price you're asking," Perley says, "I just don't know if I can swing it on my fixed income, Richit. I'm retired now, you know."

"All the more reason for a boat. How you going fishing without a boat? How you going to enjoy being retired if you don't go fishing?"

"That's what I said to Mavis. But you know Mavis . . ."

"Oh yuh," Richit says. "I used to have a Mavis at my house only she went by Carole Anne. She could be a Mavis and a half when she got going. That last time she got so worked up about me buying the elephant gun, she Mavised herself right out the door. And she could have stayed, too, because it wasn't so many months down the road Chit Stevens decided he had to have that elephant gun for the diner—he was going for a jungle theme that year, I believe—and I was in the market for a boat, so we made a trade. What was I going to do with an elephant gun anyway? No elephants around here. And if there were, the Fish and Game wouldn't let you shoot 'em. Besides, the ammunition was hard to come by."

"I should think so," Perley says, "around here."

"It was a beauty," Richit says, nostalgic. "The barrel was three and a half feet long. All I could do to lift it. At the time, my back was acting up, so I give in and traded Chit for the boat. Course, not much more than a year later it got stole right out of my yard. Reported it to Farmers Mutual and, sure enough, homeowners covered replacement value, $400. So I collected and that was all well and good except I didn't have a boat. But winter was coming on, so that was all right, and come spring, come ice out, Kermit Perkins noticed something strange in the shallow end of the reservoir. Damned if it wa'n't my boat, swamped in four feet of water. Sue Ellen and I—that's when I was going around with Sue Ellen Curly—we ratcheted it out with a block and tackle, none the worse for wear."

"I can see that," Perley says. "Looks to be in good shape for an old boat."

"Aluminum," Richit says. "Lasts forever. The thing about this boat, though, is its history. I don't know the history from before it come to me—and it was third hand, at least, when Chit Stevens traded me for the elephant gun with the mother-of-pearl inlaid stock. It was a work of art, really."

Perley says, "What's this ding here?" He's spotted a rough spot in the hull about the size of a quarter. Looks like a hole that's been filled; the filling's thicker and shinier than the metal around it.

"Gun shot," Richit says. "The kid next door went through a phase. Shot my willow tree. Shot my shed. Shot a hole through my skivvies hanging on the line. Not all at once, but over a period of time. Then he shot my boat. I couldn't put up with that. Told his folks the willow tree would survive and the shed; and the skivvies were already past it, but that hole in the boat was a problem.

"They made the boy pay $150 damage and it was a good lesson to him. Cost me about fifty cents worth of solder to fix it, but I had no compunction at all about taking the little bastard's money. If he'd had an elephant gun instead of a twenty-two, he'd have taken out the boat and two snowmobiles right behind it. Course, the elephant gun would have probably knocked his shoulder out of its spindly little socket. I never fired it myself, but I wish now I had. Just once. Just to see. Course I would have used a bench rest. Course I would have worn a shoulder pad and ear muffs."

Perley says, "So at that point, between the insurance and the delinquent next door, you'd cleared five hundred fifty bucks on that boat."

"It's got nine lives," Richit says, "and several to go. Remember that ice storm three winters ago? Trees hanging over the road and the wind came, and those trees toppling like dominoes. A lot of people got limbs through their roofs, and crushed cars and so forth."

"We lost power for two weeks," Perley said. "You ought to heard Mavis hum. That's when we got the generator. I didn't mind lugging wood, hauling water from the brook, but I couldn't stand all that humming."

"It's hard to listen to after a while," Richit says. "Gloria was an awful hummer. Smart and strong—she could lift a hundred pound bag of goat feed to her shoulder and set it down gentle as a powder puff. But she was an awful hummer, so I had to let her go. But I was saying about the ice storm, Perley, the willow couldn't take the strain and over she went. Flattened the shed and the boat inside.

The disaster lady assessed a thousand government dollars for that rotten old shed and $500 for the boat.

Perley says, "What do you mean flattened?" The boat looks about the right shape to him. He and Richit flip it upside down for a thorough examination.

"Flattened," Richit says. "Looked like a soda can the cow stepped on. But one night, about two o'clock in the morning, I set right up in bed. Joyce said, 'What the hell is ailing you, Richit?' Nothing was ailing me. I'd had an idea how to fix my boat. She said, 'Go back to sleep, Richit.' Which I did. When Joyce said to do something, you didn't hesitate. She was a hard woman. Very strict. Wears a fellow down after awhile, all that hardness, like a stone in a rim. Eventually, it'll score the metal and upset the balance and raise havoc with your tires."

"Tires aren't cheap," Perley says. "Not even down to the Rubber Warehouse. It's all I can do to afford 'em on my fixed income."

"Next morning," Richit says, "I wedged the boat in good between the stone wall and the well house, put some muscle into the house jack, and by god, if that boat didn't pop right back into shape, slick as a bean. Course, the next summer, it was struck by lightning, but after all that boat had been through already, didn't bother it one bit. Set the grass on fire all around and it was all Joyce and I could do to hose it away from the house 'til the fire department arrived. But all it did to the boat was pop a couple rivets, which I replaced, wiped off the char with vinegar and soda. Good as new."

Mavis says: "You'll probably use that boat about as much as you use that hedge trimmer."

"That hedge trimmer was a yard sale bargain," Perley says. "It was a good trade."

"We have no hedge, Perley. And the chipper-shredder? I see a chipper-shredder in the barn but I've yet to see anything being chipped or shredded."

"Not yet. But you will as soon as I get that chain saw going."

"Hmmmph," Mavis says.

"What if I told you no money changed hands?" Perley says.

"Richit doesn't give anything away," she says.

"You remember several years ago when Chit Stevens sold the diner, moved south to Massachusetts. You remember that blunderbuss, you called it, hung on the wall over the fryolater and the time I was helping Chit pack up and he said if you can heft it, you can have it, and I hefted it."

"And it's been taking up space and collecting dust ever since," Mavis says.

"I dug it out, Mavis, and when I held that beautiful blunderbuss out to Richit in my arms like a oiled-steel baby with a cherry stock inlaid mother of pearl, his eyes about popped out of his head. 'Where the hell did you get that?' he says. And this glow come all over him, Mavis, like he was having a religious experience. He looked like a man reborn and redeemed. It warmed my heart. So I said could he throw in the little trailer? He agreed that he could. So I said could he throw in the trolling motor that needs carburetor work? He agreed that he could. Probably could have gotten the life jackets, too, and the fire extinguisher, but I didn't want to take advantage of the man."

Mavis says, "What's the point of having a fishing boat, Perley, if you don't use it? You're not going fishing. That boat's going to sit out in the backyard and the rain is going to rain on it and the birds are going to poop on it and the squirrels build nests and I'm going to have to mow around it and—"

"That's where you're wrong, Mavis. For one thing, I'm going to store it in the barn next to the chipper-shredder. For another, I am going fishing. In fact, I already made plans to go hornpouting down to the reservoir on Thursday. Want to come?"

"No," Mavis says.

"That's all right," Perley says. "I'm taking Richit." ❧

# Evil Earl, Septic Man: A Saga in Five Parts

## *Preface*

SOLIDS

When the selectman got reported for above-ground flow by an irate neighbor (with whom he had a history of bad blood dating to the Big Ash Boundary Dispute of 1987), the *Woodford Ledger* got wind of the scandal and printed an exposé: *Human Waste on Candle Street—Pedestrians Beware.* It wouldn't have been such a big deal if there hadn't been a selectman involved. Selectmen are supposed to behave. It wouldn't have been such a big deal either, if there hadn't been solids.

The selectman fired off a letter to the editor. The health officer *claimed* the drainage ditch contained human waste, but how did she know? You can't always tell by looking. And the tests weren't even back yet from the state lab. Second, how did she know the source? His wasn't the only house on Candle Street, and it happened to be located at the bottom of a hill. Wasn't it possible the questionable material had washed down the hill in a rainstorm and actually belonged to the Reverend Mr. Claus Titbaum at the parsonage, or perhaps the source was Grace Church itself, diagonal across the street? Wasn't it possible that the questionable material had been planted for political purposes—by a sore loser perhaps, or a Democrat? Furthermore and finally, he, the selectman, did not in actuality *own* said property on Candle Street—so, once again, the *Ledger* had got it wrong.

Turns out the deed was in the selectman's wife's name, so technically she owned the property. Still, some reasoned, those solids, more than likely and at least in part, belonged to the selectman, so why all this talk of libel and lawsuits? Just what Woodford needed, some said, another goddamned lawsuit.

The *Ledger* printed a correction in large print on the front page with a photograph of the selectman in the Old Home Day Parade perched on a lawn chair in the bed of Neil French's

Model T truck waving a small flag. The *Ledger* also printed photographs of the selectman's wife's house, the Reverend Claus Titbaum out front of Grace Church looking constipated, and a close-up of the ditch containing what appeared to be solids but could have been wet pinecones.

Years later, it's still hard for some to pass the selectman's wife's house without smirking. Personal experience has made others more sympathetic, for example, if it's your septic stinking up the neighborhood this time around. Oh yeah—it goes around, it comes around, and sooner or later it stinks. A failed septic system is an ignominious thing—that's Greek for nasty. If you don't believe me, ask that ex-selectman or his ex-wife, Patricia.

## *Part I*

### 'BOUT LIKE CAMPIN'

It has been raining for years, seems like millennia, but your wife says four days. You cross the sponge that used to be lawn but now looks more like a mud flat (are those night-crawler holes poking up through or clam pocks?). You approach the pit, plant your feet, and lean like a stop sign clipped by a snowplow. Now you can see the whole of the Grand Canyon, the Great Depression; if it doesn't stop raining soon, it'll be Lake Winnipesaukee Junior.

A concrete tank lies on its side, cracked, as though an enormous chick tried and failed to peck its way out. A second tank lists like the Titanic. And a length of plastic pipe about the round of a telephone pole lies half-buried in the mud, stiff as a snake with rigor mortis.

There's a man in the hole, too. A big man, six feet plus, two-fifty plus, but compared to the pit he could be a gnome. Hands on hips, muck to his knees, he straddles rigor mortis. His Caterpillar cap and quilted shirt are soaked through, dark and heavy with water. He squints through rain-scoured glasses, deflects the rivulet streaming down his nose with the back of his hand. When he tries to move, the muck holds him with the suction of a brand-new, top-of-the-line Electrolux. He tries again, lurching with all his considerable weight. The muck lets go. He's face down in it.

After a while, he raises on his elbows, rolls onto his back, and pulls himself into a sitting position.

"How you doing, Reggie?" you ask.

He grins now. The rain pelts his upturned face. He grins with the innocence of a cherub, the inner confidence of a man unconscious of his own limits. "Welp," he says, "'Bout like campin'."

## *Part II*

### HUMAN NATURE

It is not, in general, a smart idea to pick your septic system installer out of the classifieds. What you should do is get a recommendation from somebody who's had work done and is satisfied. Then hire the guy who did it. But admitting to a punky roof or shaky foundation is one thing. Septic troubles? That's another thing altogether. It's embarrassing to admit your tank's backed up, your leach field plugged, gray water geysering out of the herb garden every time you do a load of wash. This is not a problem you're inclined to bring up standing in line at the bank or over ham and eggs at Harley's. Especially if, like the selectman with solids, you've let the problem slide.

You try to ignore the swamp smell that's not a swamp smell, yet it hangs in the air after a rain, sometimes when it hasn't rained. You ignore it as best you can for as long as you can, but there comes a time—the Reverend Mr. Claus Titbaum might call it the time of reckoning—when even the neighbors you get along with are snapping their windows shut against the breeze on which the stench of humanity wafts. They don't say anything, but you know what they're thinking. They're thinking you should stop being so damned cheap and shell out for a new septic.

Still, it's natural to put the expensive-thing-that-must-be-done off as long as the toilet flushes most of the time. Eventually, though, you realize even the neighbors you get along with are thinking of making anonymous phone calls to the Health Department. And the worst part? So is your wife. Action must be taken. You don't want any solids floating around in your ditches. That would be ignominious.

But instead of asking around to get the poop on who's reliable and who's not, what do you do? You check the classifieds. You make a few phone calls, get ballpark estimates, and hire the cheapest guy.

This would be Earl.

"So long as you get the thing done before the heavy frost," you say. "We don't want to drag this out all winter."

"Oh yuh!" Earl rubs his buzz cut for luck. "No problem."

You shake hands on the deal even as the thought niggles: Maybe we should put this in writing.

But Earl drives a new Chevy pickup with a magnetic sign: Earl's Septic—Get Rid of the Stink in a Wink. Only a successful entrepreneur (that means a guy with at least two jobs) could afford a truck like that. He's jolly, too, and appears enthusiastic about his work. Also, he has wide-apart eyes that hardly ever blink. Your grandmother said never trust a man with close-together eyes; on the flip side, a man with wide-apart eyes that hardly ever blink must be trustworthy indeed.

"Careful of the lilacs," you say. "My wife's great-grandmother on her father's side planted them."

Earl says, "Susie and I" (he calls his backhoe "Susie") "will snake right in-between them lilacs, dig the pit, build the leach field plenty high for a gravity drain. You got kids? It'll make a dandy sliding hill come winter, that leach field. Put in a luge run. It'll be a beautiful thing. Then, a-course, we'll get everything smoothed right out—" Earl has thrown back his big square head and gazes toward heaven. "Spread the loam, seed it in, and we're golden!" He's a man with a vision.

Plus, he's cheap.

Your wife raises her brutally plucked eyebrows when you relay Earl's quote. Low overhead, you explain. He doesn't have an office or even, as far as you can tell, a phone. The number in the classifieds was his brother-in-law's. Experienced, too. He's worked in bony ground, hardpan, clay, and even solid ledge by the sea, down to Rye where the rich people live. Putting in a septic system for a man with Earl's experience is easy as pie. And pie's real easy once you get the apples peeled. If you know how to make a crust that rolls nice. If your oven holds the heat. You don't need a fancy contract to make a pie.

"Hop to it, Earl," you say. "And here's a check for half, as requested, so you can buy materials."

"I'm on it," Earl says. "Me and Susie will be here bright and early Saturday."

Three weeks later you're thinking maybe Earl meant "a Saturday" as opposed to "this coming Saturday," because he and Susie have not yet made an appearance. Your wife has started calling him Mr. Invisible. She can be awful sarcastic, your wife.

Then one day several hundred feet of perforated pipe appear in the side yard, piled like pickup sticks.

"My rhododendron!" your wife laments.

"Maybe it'll pop back."

"It's flattened," she says. She suggests you call Mr. Invisible, determine when or if he's planning to make another appearance. And while you're at it, tell him to deduct the price of that rhododendron from the bill.

You hate to nickel and dime the guy to death, especially considering the rock-bottom deal he's giving you mainly because you seem like such a nice fella. Nevertheless, you leave a message on his brother-in-law's machine. Earl never does call back, but a week later a load of gravel appears. Earl, like Santa, does his work when nobody's around to see. You turn into the driveway to park in your regular spot, but a mountain of gravel rises before you. It blocks the garage door. That's all right. You don't park in the garage anyhow (unless it's a hurricane). You keep your tools in the garage. Sometimes you build things with your tools. You like to build things. You like the idea of building things. You're thinking about building a gazebo on top of the new leach field.

"I guess the gravel fairies came," your wife says. "When do you suppose the backhoe fairies are going to show up? You know I can't even use the dishwasher any more."

"Why not?"

"You don't want to know."

You're elected vice president in charge of washing dishes by hand. You measure time by the generations of dirty dishes waiting to be cleaned. Thirty-three generations later, a second mountain appears near the first. Then, quite suddenly, a third. Your yard is the Himalayas. You park between the mailbox and K2. A mountain of sand rises over the old septic. No way the gray water's going to bubble up through that. "Now we can do the wash in the middle of the day," you say to your wife, "instead of waiting until the dead of night like we been doing. We got pipe. We got gravel. We got sand." What you don't say is: Earl's got our money, but we got no Earl, and we got no new septic.

At the Gas and Go, Alan Ramshackle says, "Drove by your place the other day, couldn't hardly see the house. I never see so much sand and gravel outside of a pit. What you aiming for, the Mohave Desert?"

"Giza," you say.

"What'd you call me?"

"Giza—that's the town in Egypt with the pyramids."

"Oh," he says.

Eventually Earl hauls two cement tanks and the pump in on a flatbed, backs it through the Kyber pass, and there it sits for the three weekends it takes to get the pit dug and the leach field raised. "What color candy cane you want?" he hollers to your wife from Susie's high seat. Your wife stands among the stubs of what used to be lilac bushes planted by her great-grandmother on her father's side, Adah Rose.

Earl felt awful sorry about the lilacs. He was prostrated with sorrow, so he said. But when the wheels of that flatbed sunk and spun, he had to do some fancy rocking to get it out of there—unless we wanted a flatbed lawn ornament. Unfortunately, the lilac bushes jumped in the way.

"Green or white?" he hollers. "The candy cane."

"Go to hell," your wife says.

"Green it is!"

## *Part III*

'BOUT LIKE CAMPIN' CONTINUED

Still raining. You feel like Noah. Reggie pats the side of the larger
tank. "You see this crack? It's a leaker. They ain't even connected up.
The pipe comes out of the one but it don't plug into the other. Soon
as you hit the switch on that pump, it would have been pumping
effluviums into your ground."

A gust of wind pushes a wall of rain around you, through you. It
gets Reggie, too, down in the hole.

"I'm a little concerned, Reggie," you say. "How are you going to
get out of there?"

Fortunately, the rising water dilutes the mud enough so Reggie can lever himself onto the side of the tank. He clings, spread-
eagled.

Still the rain comes.

The pit is angry.

Hungry.

And it stinks.

Is that water streaming past your corneas or a whirlpool beginning to form?

"You got a rope?" Reggie says. "Or a ladder? You don't happen to
own a derrick?"

## *Part IV*

EMERGENCY MEASURES

You finally get through to Earl on a secret cell phone number his
brother-in-law reluctantly provided.

"Gout," Earl says. "I'm laid out with the gout. It's preying on my
mind that your pit needs fill and that pipe's got to be covered if
we're going to get you going before snow flies."

You're sorry about Earl's gout, but you've got problems, too.

"Things are coming to a head here, Earl." You explain how on those rare occasions when the toilet flushes, the bathtub gurgles and burps. "We can't take showers. Can't do a wash. The motor on the dishwasher burned out six weeks ago. We've had to rent a port-a-potty, Earl. It's not a good situation."

"What you need," Earl says, "is to nurse that old septic along just a little bit longer. What you need is a stopgap measure. Course you tried the plunger? And the Ream-it-Out Liquid? You tried the snake? Wait a minute," he says, "I've got an idea!"

Per Earl's instructions, you push the hose of the air compressor deep into the toilet bowl. You click the compressor on, stand back, and wait for the clog to blow.

It does.

First it was the Himalayas in the yard, now you've got Vesuvius in the bathroom. Vesuvius erupts from the tub and the sink, then, defying physics, from the toilet itself.

It's not lava.

It's not gray water.

It is effluviums.

From the doorway, your wife says, "Oh. My. God!"

An hour later, she's headed for the car with a stuffed duffle.

"Where are you going?" you say, toweling off after the hose-down.

"Vacation," she says.

"Vacation?"

"From this!" She points at the house. "From this!" She points at the minefield of your backyard. "From you!" She shoves the cat in a box and closes the lid, tosses the box into the back seat, drives away.

You don't care. You never liked that cat anyway.

Finally, Earl shows up. His gout's in remission. But it's too late.

"Take your backhoe and your flatbed; take your shovel and your come-along, your extension cords and adz; take your galvanized pail and the three Jim Beam empties you stashed in it. Earl, I've hired another man to finish the job."

"I could finish it up this afternoon," Earl says. "Won't take no time. You'll be flushing by supper time."

"The tank's cracked, Earl."

"Touch of bondo."

"The pipe's not connected. The sand's the wrong grade. The pump binds."

"I understand," Earl says.

"My wife left me."

"I understand," Earl says.

"No, Earl," you say, "I don't believe you do."

## *Part V*

### 'BOUT LIKE CAMPIN', THE FINAL CHAPTER

"Job like this," Reggie says, "shouldn't take more than a week, maybe ten days. Course if I didn't have to take out everything the other fella put in—"

"The Evil Earl," you say. "I call him the Evil Earl."

"It'd actually be cheaper to build the whole thing from scratch," Reggie says. "I hate to say it, but it's going to cost you half again as much as it would to put the whole thing in right the first time."

"Can you do it? Will you do it, Reggie?" Your voice cracks but you do not weep. You will not weep. You sniffle a little but you do not weep.

You shake on the deal even as the thought niggles: Maybe we should put this in writing. You shake even though your mother always said, "Never hire relatives." You shake even though your wife says Reggie is lazy and demented. Or she would, if she were speaking to you. Aunt Gen assures you he's taking his meds. Also, he's found God. Well, Budda, if you want to get technical. Budda is a North Country version of Buddha. Reggie learned about Budda during his extended stay at the state facilities in Berlin. The Budda super-glued to his dashboard covers the bullet hole neatly and looks something like your Uncle Perley, if your Uncle Perley were four inches high, blue, and wearing nothing but a loincloth.

"You'll have it done by Christmas," you say. "I'd really like to be flushing by Christmas, Reggie. If at all possible." In your secret heart you're thinking maybe a working septic system combined with the spirit of the season will bring your wife back to you, sarcastic as she is, plucked eyebrows and all. You miss her. A little. The cat, however, you don't miss at all.

"Oh yeah," Reggie says as you hand him a check. "No problem. I'll be back Saturday bright and early with my little backhoe, Alice." ❧

# CRIME AND PUNISHMENT

## STAKEOUT ON HUMBLE HILL

*Some of you probably remember Chief Seavey. He was the Chief of Police for Woodford, East Woodford, North Woodford, South Woodford, Woodford Parade, and so forth for years, that is before Chief Harold took over in 1975 or was it '76. There were a couple few other chiefs between Seavey and Harold, but they didn't last long. During his tenure, Seavey pretty much had the territory covered from Winnesquid to the town of Paisley, which was the biggest town in the county in those days; course it's gone downhill since.*

*One day Chief Seavey got word over the horn from the officials down to Concord that a couple of bandits had robbed a bank, stolen a car and were believed to be heading up Woodford way. He was requested to keep watch for said bandits and apprehend if possible. "Keis," Chief Seavey said to himself when he got off the phone. (He had a habit of saying Keis when he got excited. Loosely translated it means Jesum crow.)*

*Naturally, in a situation like that, the chief called in his deputy, who at the time happened to be Willy Wilson. Some of you probably remember Willy Wilson. He was one of the Long-leg Wilsons, big tall boys, six of them, each one taller than the other. Willy was the middle boy. Anyway, Chief Seavey and Willy Wilson drove the cruiser up to the top of Humble Hill, which is the height of land in Woodford, even higher than Hosshead though some dispute it, and with a better view. From the top of Humble Hill on a clear night you can see Winnesquid to the*

47

*south, the lights of Paisley to the north, and most of Woodford, East Woodford, North Woodford, South Woodford, Woodford Parade and so forth. Chief Seavey and Willy Wilson tucked the cruiser in behind a big pine tree. By the time they got situated, night was coming on fast. There they waited. Watching.*

*They waited and waited. Talked about town affairs, the Red Sox, hornpouting or whatever it is that two policemen talk about when they get together. They waited and they kept their eyeballs peeled.*

*Eventually, Chief Seavey spotted two pinprick headlights coming fast up the valley. "I think that could be those two bandits from down Concord way," he said. It was dead of night by then, and the two officers hadn't seen any other traffic on the road for more than an hour.*

*"Yup," Willy said. "Could very well be."*

*"Yup," Chief Seavey said.*

*"What are we gonna do, Chief?" Willy said. Those headlights were getting bigger. They could hear the roar of the engine. That vehicle was moving! It was coming fast up Humble Hill.*

*Chief Seavey thought a minute. "Keis, Willy," he said, "we set right here quiet behind this big pine tree and don't move, in five minutes those bandits'll be in Paisley."*

*Same town, years before that, before the roads were paved, a car got stuck in the mud late at night. Two men in the car went to the door of the nearest house and asked for help. "Do you have an ox?" they asked Mason Adams, the owner.*

*"Yup." And he was glad to help them out.*

*So the owner and his ox pulled the car out of the mud by lantern light. The two strangers were so grateful they gave Mason a $10 bill, which was a lot of money in those days.*

*Mason noticed some holes in the side of the car. Little small holes. "Are those bullet holes?"*

*"Yes," the strangers said. "We're rum runners. But the holes aren't from the cops, they're from our competition."*

*They got in the car and drove off.*

*Later, as he told the story, and he told it many times, Mason Adams would say, "I decided not to mention I was the constable." ❧*

## How the Neighbor Earned His Nickname

WHEN STRANGERS BOUGHT the Colonial on Hosshead Hill, those who live down below—which is pretty much the whole town since Hosshead represents the height of land—especially those who live at the foot of the hill in the area called the Hoof, referred to him as the Neighbor and to her as Mrs. Neighbor, even though they had different names on the mailbox, so maybe they weren't married at all. Live and let live, that's the attitude in Woodford, pretty much, particularly in the Hoof.

On the other hand, some of us were none-too-happy when the Neighbors posted their land about ten minutes after they moved in: NO TRESPASSING. NO HUNTING. NO FISHING. NO TRAPPING. DON'T EVEN THINK ABOUT PICKING A BLUEBERRY.

On the other hand, the Neighbor was none-too-happy about what happened to his chickens. It wasn't malicious or intentional; it was, however, inevitable.

I don't know what he thought he was doing when he erected that flimsy wire pen—three feet high, no top, and not even dug down in the ground. An owl could have swooped in and picked off those little peckers one at a time for a midnight snack. Or they might have fell prey to a fisher-cat or a fox or a coyote, any number of predators. It wouldn't take a coon more than a minute to finger open that paperclip latch and saunter in through the gate.

But in the end, it didn't turn out to be any of the above that did in the Neighbor's doomed chickens. Unfortunately for Randy Hickey, it was his dog, Mutt.

At first Randy denied Mutt's involvement vigorously. Mutt was home all night of the night in question, sleeping under the porch. An old dog, arthritic, a great waddling scruff of a barrel-chested St.

Bernard Newfoundland cross with a smidge of Bassett in the legs, Mutt hardly ever left the yard.

"Look at him," Randy Hickey said to Chief Harold and Officer Fred when they showed up at his doublewide investigating. "Does that look like a dog who'd ford the brook in high water, run a mile uphill through the woods, and massacre a dozen chickens in the dead of night?"

Mutt lay splayed like a rug on the kitchenette floor, under house arrest, pending. "What have you got to say for yourself, Mutt?" Officer Fred asked.

"Mutt was seen," the Chief said. "He was seen at the scene of the crime."

"Mutt was said to have been seen," Randy Hickey said. "But that don't mean he was seen. How could the Neighbor see a black dog in the dark on a moonless night?"

"Flashlight?" the Chief suggested.

Officer Fred raised Mutt's chin so they could look each other in the eye. "Did you go on a rampage?"

Mutt rolled over for a belly rub.

He and Randy maintained innocence right up until Chief Harold shined a light under the porch and Officer Fred raked out a pile of feathers, feet, bits and pieces of carcass which, reassembled, did look something like a dead chicken or two.

"It'll cost you five hundred dollars, Randy," Chief Harold said. "You pay for the Neighbor's chickens, and Mutt can walk away from this incident with impunity."

"Impunity my ass. Where am I going to get five hundred dollars? What the hell kind of chickens were they?"

"Exotic," Chief Harold said.

"Silkies," Officer Fred said. "And Frizzles."

To prepare for his meeting with the Neighbor to discuss the situation, Randy practiced looking sad and sorry in the shaving mirror as he scraped away stubble. He wasn't sad and sorry. He was POed. It wasn't Mutt's fault the Neighbor didn't know enough to build a decent pen. It's in a dog's nature to eat a chicken if the opportunity flaunts itself, just as it's in a man's nature to resent having to pay five hundred dollars for another man's Silkies and Frizzles. *Silkies and Frizzles my ass,* Randy thought, *probably garden-variety pullets.*

It was foggy in the Hoof that day as Randy started up the hill. He was walking cross-country for his health, but mostly because he couldn't get his truck sprung from the garage until he paid the balance on the valve job. In the lowlands the morning mist still hadn't burned off—and probably wouldn't for a week or two. But high on Hosshead Hill the sun shone bright.

Randy sank into the plush of a sofa so soft and low that once he finished sinking, he was staring at his own camouflage knees. He set his NRA cap like sculpture on the polished slab coffee table. Mrs. Neighbor offered herb tea. Something in the pitch of her voice made Randy's left eye twitch. She held out a platter of cookies the size of Table Talk pies. "Homemade," she said. "Oatmeal, wheat germ, soy milk, and carob chips. Bound with raisin puree."

"Yuh," Randy said. "Uh-huh." But he was thinking *skeet.*

Mercifully, she went away. The Neighbor pulled a fifth of Wild Turkey from a secret compartment in an armrest. He poured a healthy shot in each of their cups, and topped it off with hot water from the pot and a dip of honey.

"Toddy," he explained.

It wasn't half bad. The second round wasn't bad at all. The third was downright tasty. Randy began to warm to the notion that maybe the Neighbor wasn't such a bad egg after all.

"Too bad about your chickens," Randy said.

"I liked those chickens," the Neighbor confessed.

"Ain't it funny," Randy said, "how attached we get?" He meant Mutt.

"Just doing what dogs do, I guess," the Neighbor said, which struck Randy as remarkably reasonable under the circumstances. Thus inspired, he let it be known that he accepted the fact that on account of the evidence found under his porch by Chief Harold and Officer Fred, all indications were that his dog, Mutt, had mutilated several Silkies and Frizzles, therefore some amount of reparation was due. Though five hundred dollars seemed a dite steep. Besides which Randy didn't have five hundred dollars or any hope of getting five hundred dollars any time soon. "I'm strapped," he said. "I've had to buy my own doublewide back three times from my ex-wives."

Through the window they could see that the fog from the Hoof had crept up Hosshead Hill and transformed itself into a drizzle. It was drizzling all over the Neighbor's golf-course green expanse of lawn. Randy and the Neighbor sipped their toddies and stared into the drizzle. They seemed to be at an impasse.

Eventually, the Neighbor pointed to a tree that had fallen just at the point where lush lawn touched unruly woods. The trunk, Randy guessed, must be three and a half feet through. It was the biggest of its kind he'd ever seen. Must be the fertile soil and abundant sunshine on Hosshead Hill promoted unusual growth. The weathering where the bark had stripped away indicated the tree had been dead long before it fell, shattering limbs, scattering branches. It was kind of a mess, that corner of the Neighbor's near-perfect lawn.

"Maybe you could clean it up for me," the Neighbor said. "Cut it up for firewood. We've got two wood stoves and three fireplaces."

"You want me to work up that tree for firewood?" Randy said.

"Cut it to length, split it, stack it if you will, and we'll call it even."

"You sure?" Randy said.

They shook on it.

"Mutt," Randy said, once he'd staggered home. "We're talking impunity."

Mutt was glad to hear it and even gladder to get his supper, which was late.

The woodpile Randy Hickey created from the fallen tree became, for a time, a source of considerable interest in town. I believe I was the first to accept Randy's invitation to take a ride up the hill for a good close look.

"I've seen woodpiles before," I said. "What's so great about this one?"

We pulled off the road at the edge of the Neighbor's property. Didn't dare get out of the truck on account of all the No Trespassing signs. Randy handed me a pair of binoculars. "Look close now." I rolled down the window and zoomed in on the pile.

"You're looking at $500 worth of poultry right there," Randy said, proud.

"And is the man satisfied?"

"He will be," Randy said, "until he tries to burn it."

All that fall, locals made pilgrimages up Hosshead Hill just to get a look at Randy Hickey's five hundred dollar woodpile. One guy, they say, drove all the way from Winnisquam and took a picture.

Here's the best part. The strangers who bought the Colonial on Hosshead Hill are no longer called the Neighbor and Mrs. Neighbor—which is a little sarcastic, don't you think, in light of all those No Trespassing signs, a little cold.

A little cold is what they'll be if they try to heat that big house with the cordwood from Randy Hickey's five hundred dollar woodpile. Some call that particular breed of poor-burning wood Quaking Aspen. It's famous for having about as much heat in a log as in a stick of chewing gum. Some call it Poplar. Around here we call it Popple.

And that's the story of how the Neighbor earned a new nickname, which means we're warming up to him already. Another four or five years, the natives will start saying "Hey" to him at the dump. After a decade, heck, he could run for selectman and he might even get a couple of votes. On the ballot, if he's smart, along with his given name he'll list his nickname—Popple. We call him Popple and her Mrs. Popple, though neither wears a ring and they've got different names on the mailbox, so who knows. Neither of them seems to have a job, but they have plenty of money. Kind of suspicious, but none of our business. Those of us who live in the Hoof don't have time to worry about such things. We're right out straight getting our own red oak and rock maple cut, split, stacked, and snugged under a tarp. We're right out straight bracing ourselves for the long, cold, inevitable winter. ❧

# *Thief*

I'D SPOTTED THE pink sweatshirt with glittering Santa clear across the parking lot. Slush to our ankles from snow melting. Luckily I was wearing rubbers, but she had just thin sneakers and sweat pants like wicks. I grabbed a handful of glittering Santa. "Let me go," the thief said. But I had her dead to rights. Like a bull terrier, my Frank used to say, once Bunny gets her teeth into something she snarls and bites, and she won't let go.

"Where is it?" I snarled.

She tried to twist free. Didn't do any good. The shirt stretched, but my hand was a vice, clamped tight. She slapped at me. Missed. Twice my size, but no strength in her, no conviction. Marshmallow woman. Ear muffs set crooked on her head, red-gray hair tangled in the plastic band. Her eyes filled and began to leak over pink, tennis-ball cheeks.

"Listen," I said, "there's treasures in that pocketbook can't be replaced."

The sweatshirt had given her away, led me right to her. *If you're going to thief*, I thought, *you shouldn't dress so gaudy*. "Give me my pocketbook right now," I said. "Or else!"

In Bargi-Mart, I'd turned my back on my shopping cart to dig through the bin of fuzzy slippers for a pair of blue elephants with curly trunks, Beany's size. Had to dive in, because the small elephants were buried under big elephants, medium elephants, ducks, dinosaurs and bears. When I surfaced, the cart was gone and my pocketbook in the kid seat was gone too.

"Oh my Lord!" I looked up and down the aisle for Cousin Lil. "Lil?" I bleated. "Lil!" But she was across the store in bed-and-bath looking for a new bathroom scale because hers lied so. No Lil in sight, I hurried to the Courtesy Desk. But, wouldn't you know, this girl had sliced herself on an aluminum gutter in hardware, sliced right through her nylon stockings into her calf. "Could I borrow a band-aid?" she asked the clerk. But the clerk had no band-aid.

Associates congregated. "Gauze?" the girl said. "How about a tissue and some duct tape?" The blood dribbled into her furry boot, wrapped like an angora cat around her foot.

"That's a nasty gash, sweetie pie," I said. "I'd offer you a hankie, but I've lost my pocketbook."

The congregation parted at the approach of the manager—said so on his name tag—who turned foam-green eyes on me and raised one black brow, thin and shapely as a woman's. "Is this where I go for lost and found?" I said.

"With you in a moment, ma'am," he said. Then, "Larry, run to cosmetics and pull some gauze, adhesive, whatever, off the shelf. Some disinfectant. A tourniquet."

Larry ran.

"Just kidding about the tourniquet," the manager said to the bleeding girl. "You're not going to pass out or anything, are you?"

"I don't think so. Is it all right if I sit down?" She sat on the tile floor which wasn't as clean as it might have been, people tracking in and out all day through the slush.

"Someone find this young lady a chair please," the manager said. Associates scurried.

Then to me, with a sigh, "Yes, ma'am. How can I help you?" His brows drew together to make a V like the ones Beany draws for seagulls in his pictures of the ocean. Something about those eyebrows and the thought of Beany and my missing pocketbook full of treasures affected me. Like a big old baby about to cry, I said, damply: "The small elephants were way down the bottom of this great huge bin. I don't know how a short person is supposed to reach. Had to practically climb in, and when I finally extricated myself and got righted around, my cart was gone and so was my pocketbook!"

"That's terrible," the girl said, trying to contain the flow of blood with her fingers. She wiped them on her denim skirt, making four wet stripes.

"Maybe we should call an ambulance?" an associate offered.

"No, no, no," the girl said. "I'm fine."

"Has anybody turned in a purse in the last ten minutes?" the manager called out to associates at large.

I'd lost my money, my keys, my driver's license, and my checkbook that said where I lived, so the thief could use the house key, walk right in, terrorize the little dog, and steal everything else I owned. "It was a good-sized maroon pocketbook with a lot of compartments and my initials on the flap." Mother's celluloid pillbox with my blood pressure medicine was in that purse. Also a new roll of antacids, a comb and mirror in a small plastic case. An amplified voice rolled over us from a raised cubby behind the Courtesy Desk: "No pocketbooks turned in all morning. None whatsoever."

"What'll I do?" In that pocketbook was the smooth white stone Frank found at York Beach, Maine, in the summer of 1954 that I'd carried in a velvet pouch ever since; and the laminated key-chain photo of Frank and me on our fortieth; and the wallet album with pictures of all my thirteen grandkids, including Beany, hairless from the chemo, grinning like the little imp he is. Beany's new slippers, hitched together with plastic thread, still draped my wrist. "I can't believe this," I said with a flutter of elephants that accidentally puffed the manager's chin. His brows knit, delicate as ribbons.

"Here's a chair," an associate said.

"Thank you," I said, but it wasn't for me. The associate placed the chair behind the bleeding girl. The manager lifted her into it by the armpits, her sweater mooshing up in his hands. I noticed that neither the manager nor the girl was wearing a wedding ring. *Ah ha!* I thought. *Those two are going to fall in love. Maybe.* I couldn't wait to tell Lil my premonition. She'd get a kick out of it. Lil devours two romance novels a week, minimum, the old mush.

The cashier from aisle eight called over. "I saw a pocketbook leave the store."

"Maroon?" I said.

"I think so," the cashier said. "It went out with a woman in a pink shirt with Christmas decorations, all sparkles—kind of odd for February. It went just this minute out the door. I thought it was strange because she had two pocketbooks, one in the cart and one on her shoulder."

"Pink shirt?" I said.

"Glow-in-the-dark," she said. But I'd already spotted pink through the plate glass window, a neon flash, and I was headed for the door, tripping out into the slush, sun tearing my eyes, parking lot chock full, but I caught a blur of pink crossing in front of the dark windows of the liquor store, and barreled over, dodging cars, honing in. Didn't know I could move so fast in a pinch, bad hip and all. If she saw me coming, she didn't let on. Just kept walking. She ducked behind a van. I dodged around the other side and caught her wading a puddle over a plugged drain.

"Stop right there," I said, expanding to my full height and width, which is considerable, to block her way. "You in the pink."

She tried to squeeze around me, but I grabbed a handful of that Santa shirt and wouldn't let go. She stood there at the end of my arm, limp as Raggedy Ann. "Let me go," she said. Looked like if I did let go, she'd crumple into a heap. I didn't let go. I informed her in no uncertain terms that she was going nowhere until I got my pocketbook back.

"What are you, crazy?" she said.

Crazy like a bull terrier. She tried to twist free, but not too hard, and I hung on. Stubborn runs strong in my family. It can make us miserable to live with—though Frank never said so, never dared! But it comes in handy, too, when you're fighting for your pocketbook like me, or fighting for your life like Beany. I snatched the ratty bag hanging off her elbow. The bag's strap and the elephant slippers tangled, but I wedged the bag under my chin and managed the zip with my free hand.

"That's mine," she said.

"Ha," I said, when a twenty dollar bill fell out, then a ten. I plucked out three ones creased lengthwise down the middle the way I always crease them. "What'd you do with the rest of my stuff?"

She leaned away, dead weight, as far as the shirt would stretch. I thought the sheer bulk of her might topple me, so I let go. She closed her eyes and sagged against the van, white with salt, while I dug through her stuff. I dug out a pack of Juicy Fruit, pencil stub, inhaler, a can of Baby Soft cologne rattling around with the change and mints.

But, no celluloid pillbox. No checkbook. No pictures of the grandkids. No beach stone.

*What now, Frank?* I thought, the way I do sometimes when I'm upset even though he's long gone.

"Bunny?" It was Lil, bright-eyed and righteous with that puff of white hair like a crown. She stood behind the thief, a shopping bag in one hand, the other knotted on her hip. She filled the narrow space between the van and the station wagon. "Mercy," the old mush said, "I thought you'd left me. I thought you'd forgot and left me, and I was going to have to walk all the way home. What on earth?"

"You stand right there, Lil," I said. "Don't let this one by. She stole my pocketbook."

"No!" Lil said. Then, "That's not your pocketbook, Bunny."

"It's *her* pocketbook," I said. "with my money in it." I bent to pick a bill out of the slush. "See. I always crease my dollars just this way. This is my twenty-dollar bill. This is my ten-dollar bill. See." I tucked the money and her wallet into my coat pocket, then thrust the ratty bag back at her, pressing the inhaler into her hand, so she'd have it if she needed it. Didn't want her asphyxiating herself right here in the parking lot, at least not until I got my pocketbook back.

"Should we beat her up?" Lil said, brandishing the shopping bag. "Should I rap her a good one with my new bathroom scale?"

"I didn't steal nothin'. I didn't do nothin'," the thief said. She coughed, wiped her nose on her sleeve, sucked on her inhaler.

"Drop her with a karate chop if she tries to get away, Lil," I said. "No sense denting your new bathroom scale." Lil took Self-defense for Seniors at the Tech school. She's small but wiry and she knows all kinds of tricks.

"I wa'n't nowhere near Bargi-Mart," the thief said.

"Ha," I said. "How did you know my pocketbook was stolen out of Bargi-Mart? I never mentioned the Bargi-Mart. Did I mention the Bargi-Mart, Lil?"

"Not since I been here," Lil said.

The thief drooped and closed her eyes. She wrapped her pitifulness around herself like a blanket and disappeared inside. "I didn't steal nothin'," she said. "I didn't do nothin'."

Just then, I heard a siren in the distance, way up on North Main Street sounded like. "Hear that?" I said. "They're coming for you." But she just stood there hugging her ratty bag, chin on her chest.

"I didn't do nothin'," she whispered.

"Are you sure, Bunny?" Lil said. "Are you sure you didn't just walk off and leave it like you do sometimes? Did you forget it in the rest room?" The siren in the distance grew louder, more distinct, musical.

"Didn't need to rest, Lil," I said. "Rested before we left the house, remember."

"Maybe it's still in the car," Lil said. "My goodness, remember that time you kicked it under Beany's bed at the hospital and you had us looking all over at the gift shop and the lobby and the TV room, and you thought maybe you left it at Jeanie's, and the nurse finally found it an hour later under Beany's bed?"

"I had my pocketbook in Bargi-Mart," I said. "I had it in my shopping cart, and *she* was seen leaving the store with *my* pocketbook in *my* shopping cart! The one in the pink Santa shirt with the glitter, they said. You see anybody else around here wearing a pink glittery Santa shirt?"

"No," Lil said. Then to the thief in her retired fifth-grade-teacher voice: "Where is it? What did you do with Bunny's pocketbook? You give it back right now. Right now!"

"I didn't do nothin'," the thief wailed. "Nothin'."

The siren, a rising wail itself, now sounded like it was speeding along Depot Street, rounding Pet Shop Corner. I tugged the thief's wallet from my pocket, thumbed through her cards—hands shaking, knees quaking, that's how mad I was. I read the big lettering on her library card: "Mary Elsbeth Pike." The siren throbbed, an earthquake of sound coming our way, right into the parking lot one row away. "Mary Elsbeth Pike," I said, "they're coming for you."

She stepped away from the van, salted from shoulder to hip, and danced a nervous two-step like she wanted to run but which way? At me? At Lil? Maybe throw herself over the hood of the station wagon and roll? She didn't look like she was in any shape for such acrobatics.

"My pocketbook," I said, "or else!" I smacked my fist into my palm, flailing elephants. "Oh my Lord," I said. "Beany's slippers. Lil, I never paid for them. I rushed right out of Bargi-Mart without paying. Oh my Lord, Mary Elsbeth and I might both end up in the hoosegow."

Across the parking lot, on the wide sidewalk in front of Bargi-Mart, the manager paced, coatless, hatless, up and down the expanse of concrete on the balls of his feet, rubber-necking all over for somebody, probably me, elephant thief. The ambulance siren echoed from the low, wet buildings. A cruiser wailed to a halt in front of the manager, ambulance right behind.

When Mary Elsbeth tried to squeeze between me and the station wagon, I discouraged her with a small shove, just a poke, a nudge really, but her sneakers slipped, and she plopped down in the slush on her marshmallow butt.

Pitiful.

"I'm sorry," I said, and I was. I didn't want her to hurt herself. I didn't want her to break a hip. People die from broken hips. Bending to help her up, I accidentally puffed her on the head with the elephants which tangled with her pink ear muffs. "Ow," she said.

Lil said, "You're pulling her hair right out by the roots, Bunny. Careful. You're all tangled up."

Mary Elsbeth struggled to her feet, elephants and ear muffs hanging off her head, tennis-ball cheeks flushed red, wet and salty as the rest of her. "In the trash barrel in front of the liquor store," she said without looking me in the eye. "I think I saw somebody stick a pocketbook in that trash barrel."

"My goodness," Lil said, disentangling elephants and muffs. "You're soaked to the bone."

"She pushed me down," Mary Elsbeth said.

"I didn't mean to," I said.

"She pushed me right down."

"I said I was sorry."

"I'm sorry, too," she said.

I could see that she was. Sorry she got caught!

"You stay here," I said. "Lil, watch her!"

At the trash barrel in front of the liquor store, sure enough, when I raised the flap and reached through, the first thing my fingers touched, thank God, was the familiar vinyl and raised gold lettering of my maroon pocketbook. I pulled it out, pawed through to make sure everything was intact—keys, check book, photo album, pillbox—then waved to Lil. Triumphant. She waved back. By then, God bless her thieving heart, Mary Elsbeth was halfway to Shop and Save, picking up speed, but I didn't care, as long as I had my pocketbook back.

Over at Bargi-Mart, paramedics had strapped the bleeding girl onto a stretcher and were rolling her through the automatic doors. The manager walked beside her. He wasn't holding her hand, but I could see he would have liked to. She was a pretty girl and plucky. Obviously, she had bled her way into his lonely heart. "It's nothing," she said. "It's really nothing. Look, I'm hardly bleeding at all anymore."

"You just lay still," he said, "and let these people take care of you."

"Excuse me," I said to the manager, "I accidentally stole these slippers, but I'm going to go back in and pay for them, because you'll be happy to know I located my pocketbook."

"Isn't that lucky," the bleeding girl said as they slid her into the ambulance. I wondered if they were taking her to Beany's hospital. Probably. If so, maybe we'd run into her over there.

In the car, Lil said, "She'll be fine."

"They'll fix her right up," I said. "A few stitches, tetanus shot, what have you. She'll be all set."

"He's smitten," Lil said, "that young man. The manager with the pretty eyes. Don't you think?" She's such an old mush. I didn't answer her, because I was up to my elbow in my pocketbook, groping for keys. Finally located them, but in the process realized I couldn't feel the velvet pouch with the smooth beach stone in its usual place. "Oh no," I said, digging frantically through the uncharted depths of the middle compartment.

"What's wrong?" Lil said.

"My special stone," I said. "I can't find it."

"That's all right, Bunny," Lil said. "How 'bout we drive to the beach and get you another one."

*Not the same*, I thought. *Not Frank's; not the stone Frank found special for me at York Beach, Maine, in 1954.*

Then I touched it, the velvet bag. I felt the shape and weight of the stone inside. Then I had it safe in my hand.

"Whew," I said. "For a minute I thought we were going to have to turn that trash barrel out on the sidewalk and pick through."

I opened the pouch, held out my hand, palm up, and let the stone fall into it. I let it roll cool and healing over my winter-chapped skin: my lucky stone, a perfect stone, a stone as smooth and round as Beany's dear little bald head. ❧

# *Snip*

BIRD PINS THAT sparkle, I collect them. One this big, this peacock (ain't it delicate?), technically it's a brooch. I don't wear it much—special occasions.

Vintage. Like me. In our family, we're all collectors of one thing and another. When we get together, first thing anybody says: "What are you collecting these days?" Salt cellars, buttons, shot glasses, jokers—not the whole set of playing cards, just the jokers. Stamps, coins, postmarks, of course. Did you know the most valuable postmark in the world, far as I know, was stamped in Boscawen, just up the road? Wouldn't I like to get my hands on one of those? My brother Joe collects guns. All the men collect guns, pretty much, but Joe's got the biggest collection by far. Some collect tools. Pocket knives. One of Myra's twin boys collects dump trucks. That's Eli. Toy trucks, yes, but also the real deal. Eli had five in his dooryard at one time, only one with any hope of starting. He's divorced, three times. Myra says the dump truck collection didn't help.

Her other twin boy, Roy, collects culverts.

Collecting, you might say, runs in the family. Do you collect anything special?

So what brings you to court today? I've never been before; it's nervous-making. Little bit. Everybody so serious and quiet. Nice suit. I like a man who wears a suit. A lot of these young men wouldn't wear a suit to their own funeral. You're not a reporter, are you? Because if you were I'd have to shut my trap and keep it shut. I've got my marching orders. Nice tie, too. Not a lawyer? If you were a lawyer, you'd be sitting up front instead of way back here with the riffraff.

He's my nephew. The defendant. Oh, it's a terrible thing to have a defendant in the family. A defendant. I never thought I'd see the day. And I tell you it's killing my sister Kathleen. Says she's holding up, doing as well as could be expected. But she ain't. She's going to pieces. Inside, you know, where it does the most damage. Oh-my-goodness, they're bringing him in now! That's pitiful. Handcuffs. Look at him: the gentlest soul I've ever known. Innocent as the day he was born. He's my sister's baby boy; known him all his life. Besides, it's all circumcisal anyway. The evidence, I mean.

That's what the lawyer told Kathleen. Roberta Bickford, that's the lawyer. Nobody *caught* him in the act *flagranty*, Roberta says, so that makes it circum-whatever. One girl says she saw something; but it was dark! How could she see anything in the pitch dark? What is she, an owl? Probably drunk, too. That's what they do at the college—drink. They're all majoring in Budweiser, that's what I hear. I never knew that boy to do anything wrong his whole life, not on purpose. When he was real small, he had a habit of biting, but he didn't know any better at the time. Of all my nineteen nieces and nephews, not counting the baby who died, he was the only biter, far as I know. He bit his sister Carole so bad in the forearm she had seven stitches. "Carole," Kathleen said, "what provoked your brother to do such a thing?"

Carole didn't know. "We was just playing Lincoln Logs, Ma, on the floor, and he rolled over and bit me for no good reason. He wunt mad or nothin'. We wunt fightin' or nothin'."

The little guy didn't seem to realize what he'd done wrong. Course, once Carole got crying, he got crying, and once Kathleen saw all that blood pouring out of her baby girl, she got crying, too. I guess it was pretty wet around town for a while. He only had the four teeth—two on top and two on the bottom. The doc was amazed he could do so much damage with just the four baby teeth. Tried to gnaw his way through an electric cord one time, but somebody stopped him before he electro-fried himself. Bit his Uncle Hooky in the nose. But if I know Hooky, he was asking for it. Bit a little girl at the beach because she tried to take his plastic shovel. She was twice his size, and Snip was just defending himself.

Oh, yes, Snip. That's his nickname. But I'm not supposed to . . . His real name's Myron after my dad. Maybe they should have called him "Nip" because he was such a little nipper. But only until he got old enough to know better. He didn't mean any harm.

No, he doesn't go to the college, though he's about the right age. Well, a little older. He's a smart boy, but not the academic type. More of a hands-on person. He works at the college. Used to, I should say. Maintenance II. They number the jobs. The higher the number the better the pay. He was working his way up the ladder. They let him go, you know. Soon as he was arrested, they said even if he made bail, he shouldn't bother to come back to work. Whatever happened to innocent until proven guilty?

He loved that job, Kathleen said. His specialty was the grounds part of Maintenance II—mowing the lawns, pruning the trees, trimming the hedges around the President's house. You ever see those hedges? Massive. You're not a teacher are you? You look like a teacher! It's the tweed and your patience, I'm noticing. Here you sit, calm as a cucumber, and I'm fidgeting all over, talking up a storm, when I should be keeping my big mouth shut. You sure you're not a reporter?

When that lawyer, Roberta Bickford, asked me—she talked to all the relatives—to describe Snip in one word, I said "helpful." Give you an example. One summer I come into an awful lot of string beans. Course I could have left them for shell, but to me a shell bean is too dry, even swimming in its own juice. Sn—, I mean, Myron, stopped by and we sat at the round table under the umbrella listening to the radio, snapping beans all one afternoon. He was a teenager at the time and liked that pound-pound-wail-wail music. I didn't mind so long as he didn't play it too loud. Course I prefer the country-western. Real country-western: Loretta Lynn, Johnny Cash, Tanya Tucker, cute little thing with a great big voice. She was married to somebody famous, who wasn't anywhere near as good a singer as her. Glen Campbell, that's right. The Wichita Lineman! They got divorced. They all get divorced eventually. Practically everybody in my family who's ever been married has got divorced. Except my folks. They died married. Some of us avoid the whole issue by staying single. Me, for example. And Myron. Course, he's young yet. Anyway, we sat under that umbrella all one hot afternoon snapping beans. I snapped. He cut off the ends with a little pair of shears. Click click, click click. Throw the ends into a bucket for mulch and the beans into the colander. Imagine that strapping teenage boy—he had his full growth by the time he was fourteen, over six feet tall and, oh my gosh, at least 200 pounds, but very light on his feet—imagine that big boy sitting there all afternoon snapping beans with his Auntie, content as a cat.

Afterwards, I said, "Snip, let's you and me go in the house and treat ourselves to a big bowl of maple walnut ice cream with cool whip." Why you'd think that maple walnut ice cream was nectar.

"This is the best ice cream I ever had, Auntie." And, "This is just about the nicest day ever."

Excuse me while I get a tissue. I get a little weepy thinking about things and wondering how this whole big mess came about. I feel bad for the boy, of course. But even worse for my sister Kathleen. Family, you know.

Snip appreciates family, appreciates the small things in life, like string beans on a hot summer afternoon and maple walnut ice cream. He wasn't tough, like some of the other boys. Even though he'd had a tough life. His father, Dick, I call him Dick-who-lives-up-to-his-name, abandoned that little family about two minutes after Snip was born. He left Kathleen and all those kids and her trying to recover from a botched C-section. I call it botched; the lawyers couldn't prove it, unfortunately. This place is lousy with lawyers, ain't it. Everybody so serious. All these long faces. Makes me feel like laughing. I don't know about you, but when I get nervous, I laugh. Can't help it. Better laugh than cry, that's what I say. Gets me into trouble sometimes.

My sister Kathleen wasn't right for a year after that botched C-section. I don't think she ever got over it really. Twenty-eight years later and she still gets pains down there. That's her and Dick, the backs of their heads in the second row. She's got her hair twisted up in that thick braid tight to her head. That's right. The largish woman in the green cowl-neck sweater.

Dick's the one with the long bald head, looks sort of like an albino zucchini only red at the neck. He has high blood pressure. If he turns around you'll see the red in his face and his flat veiny nose. Sounds like a drinker, I know, but I don't believe it. Course, I didn't believe he would desert Kathleen with those five little kids and a botched C-section to contend with. And for no good reason, far as I know. It wasn't another woman or drugs or being gay or anything like that, far as I know. He packed his bags, moved to an apartment in Manchester and that was it. Kathleen was some startled and upset. We all were.

66

Course you never know what goes on behind closed doors. Or inside somebody's head for that matter. And if Dick thought a piddly little child-support check once a month made up for no daddy in the house, you ask any of those kids and they'll tell you, it does not.

Kathleen never remarried. Neither did he. So why didn't he just stay put? At least until the kids were grown. And there they sit, side-by-side, like an old married couple, putting up a united front. You married? Kids?

Myra's oldest twins, Eli and Roy, are, oh gosh, going on fifty, but they're still her babies. They'll always be her babies. Same with Kathleen and Snip. He's her big little boy. She wanted him to be a doctor. Thought he'd make a great surgeon on account of he was so nimble with his fingers from a very young age. Hand-and-eye coordination. Excellent hand-and-eye coordination. All his teachers said so. They said he had manwell dexterity. But that manwell dexterity got him into trouble, too, from time to time. That's the thing. He hand-and-eye coordinated the heads off Grammie's peonies. Wa'n't she ugly. Nobody told him the difference between the flowers to cut for a vase and the ones to leave alone. He did enjoy practicing his hand-and-eye coordination. He practiced on his cousin Maureen's beautiful pink curls. Yes, pink. Real blonde with just a hint of red, so in a certain light they looked pink. And so thick Lucille practically had to sedate her to draw a comb through. Snip said Maureen asked him to give her a haircut and Maureen agreed that she had, but Lucille didn't believe it. Strange thing, when Maureen's hair grew back it wasn't curly any more or pink either. She didn't give a hoot, but I don't think Lucille ever got over it. Course, Lucille's own hair is straight as a stick and brown.

Ha! I'm just remembering—and it makes me laugh—remembering how that little devil cut the tassels off all Kathleen's couch cushions. And her rugs. Didn't hurt the rugs any, but Kathleen was fit to be tied, because she'd specifically told him to leave those tassels alone. He couldn't resist tassels. Course it's not so funny when it happens to you. I'll never forget that sweet round face, those big eyes looking up at me: "Sorry, Auntie," after he cut every last string on the Venutian blinds in the sun room and there they lay in a pile. I said, "You sit right there in your Grandfather's chair and don't you get up until you've thought about what you did to those Venutian blinds, because now I've got to get new ones or people will be looking in the windows at night when we're watching television. Venutian blinds are expensive."

You know what he said. He said: "You could get some shades, Auntie. Or some curtains." Then he said, again, that he was sorry, awful sorry. He looked sorry coming into court today. And he is, I know. He's sorry for the lies they're saying about him! Sorry for what they're saying he did, based on practically nothing but circumcisal evidence. And scared, too. They said he sneaked into those girls' rooms and . . . well, whoever sneaked in and sliced the nighties and underclothes off those sleeping co-eds without a single nick or scratch, that person certainly did have a good deal of manwell dexterity. But it wasn't him. Couldn't have been. They're calling it a crime of sexual something or other, but anybody who knows that young man knows he's never had a girlfriend in his life. Never had much interest in girls at all. Or—I know what you're thinking—boys either. He was content keeping to himself. I understand that. I'm the same way. I'd rather have a nice caramel and a cup of pepmint tea, call it a day.

Oh—Kathleen's trying to talk to him, but they won't let her. That's just cruel. She's talking to Roberta Bickford instead. That's Roberta Bickford in the dazzling blue suit with the short-short hair. She must get it cut once a week to keep it so trim. She's supposed to be real good. Maybe if Kathleen had Roberta for a lawyer after her botched C-section, she'd have got some money out of it. To this day she gets pains down there like somebody's pinching her from the inside. The docs can't seem to do anything for her. Probably think it's all in her head. Psycho-something. Maybe she should try that psycho-ologist Snip's seeing. Maybe they could get a family rate! Except she doesn't believe in psycho-ology any more than I do, which is to say it's a bunch of baloney, and that's the polite term. Roberta Bickford says the psycho-ologist might be able to get Snip off by saying he was compulsed and couldn't help himself. That's where the nipping and snipping since childhood comes in, you see.

Shouldn't they be starting up soon? I don't know if I have time to pop out to the ladies room or not. They can't start until the judge gets here, though, can they. Roberta Bickford likes this judge. She has a boy of her own about Snip's age, which is a good thing. Oh, here she comes now, all decked out, the judge. Don't she look strict? Don't she look like she got up on the wrong side of the bed?

Truth be told, and just between us, I'm worried. It's all circum-cisal evidence, but *if* he sneaked in the night through some un-locked doors or wide-open windows—which were practically an invitation—*if* he passed through those unlocked doors or windows and snipped those underclothes off those sleeping co-eds, the fact is he never hurt them, not a nick or a scratch, didn't even wake them up except one, who says he did, but she could be lying.

If he did what they said he did, which I don't believe he did, he wasn't just snipping, he was collecting.

You see. We're all collectors in the family. It was the collecting, if anything, got him into trouble. It was those bits and pieces of un-derwear and so forth they found all wobbed up in a suitcase at the back of his closet that got everybody so suspicious. Still, Roberta Bickford says . . . Oh, look, the judge is sitting down and Roberta's standing up. Looks like we're about to get going.

What did you say your interest was in this case? You come all the way from Pennsylvania to sit in this lemon-wax courtroom. Nice day like this, you could be out admiring the foliage. Unless, you just enjoy the drama. Unless . . . you say you have a daughter? And she goes to the college. *Used* to.

Oh dear. Now I've gone and put my foot in it. Oh I'm sorry, I mean I'm—I don't know what I mean. Blathering on. And they told me to keep my mouth shut. They said, Auntie, you can come to the court, but sit in the back and keep your mouth shut. And whatever you do, don't say anything about Sn—, I mean, Myron. Ha! I don't mean to laugh . . . I really don't . . . Sometimes I get laughing. Laughing . . . I don't know why. Nothing's funny. Not one thing. It's just . . . sometimes I get compulsed, sometimes I just can't help myself. ❧

# WILDLIFE

*On the highway heading into Paisley, you pass a series of ponds all in a row, kind of scenic. They're not ponds though, they're lagoons. Sewage treatment lagoons. Driving by, a Paisley resident was surprised to see an SUV with Massachusetts plates pulled up kind of close to the middle lagoon. Nearby crouched two men in full fatigue, with shotguns. Duck hunters.*

*"Duck hunters?"*

*"Yup," the resident said. "Duck hunters." She added: "I felt awful sorry for that retriever."* ℁

*Hermit Island is a big camping area on Casco Bay, near Bath, Maine. People come from all over to set up their tents on sites overlooking the ocean or even right on the beach. It's very popular and has been for decades. The thing about Hermit Island, it's not an island, it's the tip of a peninsula—or as they say in Maine, a spit. From the tar road, you drive on a raised gravel road across a tidal flat to get to the Kelp Shed, where you check in and nice people direct you to your campsite.*

*A woman from an inland state, maybe Kansas, drove in one evening around sunset, was given a map of all the little roads on the island. X marked the spot where she would set up her tent. She went off and all seemed well, until the next morning when she came tearing into the Kelp Shed demanding to talk to somebody important. Apparently somebody important showed up, and she launched into her complaint.*

*"I paid for a waterfront site," she said. "But out in front of my tent it's nothing but mud as far as the eye can see."*

*"Well," Somebody Important said. "There's the tide to consider. You know about the tide."*

*"Of course I know about the tide," the woman said. "I'm talking about mud."*

*"Well, ma'am," Somebody Important said. "The tide comes in and the tide goes out. The tide went out. You have to understand, ma'am, every day the tide goes out. You know about the tide going out? Right?"*

*"Of course, I know the tide goes out," the woman huffed. "I didn't know it took the water with it."* ॐ

*Mrs. O taught kindergarten in a very small New Hampshire town, which shall go unnamed. One morning at circle, she asked the children what they'd had for supper the night before.*

*Susie said: "We had hot dogs and beans with mustard."*

*Jim said: "We had macaroni and cheese. I like macaroni and cheese."*

*Billy said: "We had venison stew made from the deer hanging in my daddy's barn."*

*Mrs. O said, "I don't think the deer's still hanging in your daddy's barn, Billy. It's February."*

*"Oh yes it is," Cheryl piped up. "There's seven of 'em in there and two of 'em my daddy's."* ॐ

## THE DIFFERENCE BETWEEN DURHAM AND GORHAM

*In Durham, talking about writing with a senior honors English class, I read from a story by Thomas Williams called "Horned Pout Are Evil." The students seemed puzzled. "What's the problem?" I said.*

*One kid asked, "What's a hornpout?"*

*"What do you think it is?"*

*"A bird?"*

*A week later I was in Gorham writing stories with third graders.*

*"Now, to write a story," I told them, "you need some interesting char-*
*acters." I suggested writing about some interesting animal characters*
*and asked what kinds of animals lived around Gorham. Beaver, they*
*said, raccoons, deer, moose. "Moose!" I said. "Let's write a story about*
*a moose. Now, to write well about a character, you have to know some-*
*thing about him. What's a moose like?"*

*A little boy raised his hand. "What's a moose like, Jerrod?" I said.*
*"Delicious."*

*And that's the difference between Durham and Gorham.* ❧

*Gob and his brother Walter were fly fishing on the Squam River. Walter*
*made a mighty cast, but the line flipped back on him and that Golden*
*Demon embedded itself deep in his arm. Across the river, as luck would*
*have it, was Doc Paul. He gets his bag, swabs the arm with disinfectant.*
*"I'll have to cut the hook off first," he says.*

*"Doc," Gob says, "do you have to? That's the only fly we've caught a*
*fish on all day."* ❧

*At another country doctor's office, a young patient admired Dr.*
*Bozuwa's collection of fishing lures and flies framed and hung on the*
*wall. "You must be a very good fisherman, Dr. Bozuwa," the boy said.*

*"I don't fish at all," the doctor replied. "I pulled all those out of people's*
*heads."* ❧

THE SALMON RUN

*Gert heard some shooting down by the river. This was in the spring,*
*years ago, when the amount of salmon running up that river into the*
*lake to spawn was impressive. Of course, you can't fish for salmon when*
*they're spawning. Couldn't then. Can't now. (If you're lucky enough to*
*find any.)*

*Now, in some places if you hear gunfire, you head in the other direc-*
*tion. But in New Hampshire, we sometimes get curious. Gert got curi-*
*ous. She traipsed through the woods in the direction of the shots. Heard*
*a couple more shots. Louder this time. Knew she was on the right track.*

*Pressed on. Pretty soon she comes to the river, and there's her neighbor Everett sitting on the riverbank with a .22 resting across his knees.*

*"What are you doing, Everett?" she says.*

*"Shooting muskrats," he says.*

*"Huh?" She looks and beside him on the bank among the ferns she sees four good-sized salmon, all laid out, not looking too lively.*

*"Muskrats, huh?" she says, skeptical.*

*"Yup," Everett says. "Scaley bastids, ain't they."* ❧

## Leroy: The Biggest Fish in Lupa Pond

BIG JIM AND Little Jim sit on stumps, their poles propped on forked sticks. They eagle-eye their lines because there are fish in Lupa Pond big enough to pull their poles off those forked sticks and swim away with them. The biggest of the big fish in Lupa Pond is called Leroy.

A stranger arrives, his eyes shaded by a cloth hat with feathers hooked through the brim like small birds ready for flight. He looks the situation over.

Just then Little Jim's line snakes out. He flicks the pole to set the hook and reels in a lively trout.

"Nice one!" the stranger says.

Big Jim says: "That fish is just puny compared to Leroy."

Little Jim returns the puny trout to the pond.

The stranger hikes back to his Jeep for a cooler, pretzels, and a paperback book. He slips salmon eggs on a hook like five red beads. He casts way out. His red-and-white bobber soars, the egged hook trailing like a kite tail. A breeze ruffles the water. The bobber bobs. The stranger doesn't realize trout in Lupa Pond have gone to bobber school. They know a red-and-white ball on top means a hook below.

"So what's all this about Leroy?" the stranger asks.

"I had him on a line twice," Big Jim says. "But he snaps twenty-pound test like thread. Lately, I've gone to a heavier gauge."

Little Jim claims Leroy stole his pole and dragged it all the way to Pine Point. "Which is where he would have dragged you, too, if I hadn't held you back," Big Jim says.

From the cove comes a great splash like a heron taking off.

"Leroy," the Jims say. "He knows we're talking about him."

They fish some more. After awhile, Big Jim says: "See that aluminum boat tied up to the tree? See that large dent in the side? Leroy was rounding up shiners for a snack and they bunched in the shallows. Leroy dove after them, didn't look where he was going, rammed smack into the side of that boat. Any other fish, the blow would have knocked him out on the spot. Leroy just shook his head and swam away. But the boat has never been the same."

The stranger's friend arrives in an orange VW Bug. "Hey Ned," the friend calls. It seems the stranger's name is Ned.

"Better park that vehicle well back from shore," Big Jim says. "Leroy might mistake it for a tasty orange poppin' bug."

Ned says, "Where you been, Clark? Where's your boat?"

"In my trunk," Clark says.

The Jims never knew a boat could fit in the trunk of a VW Bug. Clark pulls out a large rubber pancake and inflates it. As the pancake rises, Big Jim says: "One time two old ladies at a camp on the back side of the pond set up chaise lounges in the water so they could cool off their feet. Leroy thought those dainty toes were marshmallows."

"Trout love marshmallows," Little Jim says.

"When he swished in for a nibble," Big Jim says, "he flicked a wave that knocked those chaise lounges right over and the old ladies, too."

Clark and Ned arrange their gear in the pancake boat, including a pair of plastic oars about as long as Big Jim's forearm. They take off their shoes and socks, roll up their trousers, and wade in. Clark looks at their white feet in the water. "Ned," he says. "I think Leroy's about to bite you in the shin." He points at a fingerling circling Ned's bare leg, nibbling the hairs.

"Leroy doesn't like to be made fun of," Little Jim says.

Clark and Ned organize themselves in the pancake boat. Shadows pass over: three high-flying mallard ducks.

"Those ducks'll keep going if they know what's good for them," Big Jim says. "Leroy has been known to mistake ducks for Mayflies."

Clark and Ned tighten their life jackets.

"Cousin Russell claims to have hooked onto Leroy ice fishing," Big Jim says. "Cut a hole in the ice and dropped a hand line. Sure enough, Leroy chomped ahold of that bait and refused to let go. But Russell's stubborn. A tug-o-war ensued. We found Russell the next day, stuck tight as a cork headfirst down the hole."

"Did he drown?" Clark asks.

"No," Big Jim says. "But it didn't do him much good."

The Jims help by pushing the rubber boat into deeper water. Ned and Clark burble away. The Jims fish. All is quiet on Lupa Pond for a long time until Ned yells: "Net!" His pole bends almost in half. Ned has a bite.

Little Jim waves and Big Jim grins when the pancake boat sails by, even though it has no sails and nobody's rowing.

Ned and Clark are both holding onto that bent pole for dear life as they're dragged from one side of Lupa Pond to the other. Little Jim wonders if they should call 911, but they have no phone. Big Jim says, "Leroy's just teaching them a lesson. He'll drag them around awhile, but sooner or later he'll let them go."

Just then, as luck would have it, Big Jim gets a bite and hauls in a trout about a foot long. He draws the hook from the trout's lip and shakes his head. "Another puny one."

"Pitiful puny," Little Jim says, "compared to Leroy." ⸙

# Wrestling Destiny: A True(ish) Story Followed by A Short Quiz

DRIVING ALONG FLUTTER Street close to dusk, Pod sees the flashing lights of the town cruiser and two police officers wrestling each other by the big rock that looks like a squatting elephant or the planet Saturn, depending on whether you're driving east or west.

Naturally, Pod pulls over. Evidently the light or lack of it played a trick on him. Chief Harold and Officer Fred aren't wrestling each other. They are wrestling a large pig.

Chief Harold shouts over a porcine shoulder: "Do you know how to control a pig?" Raised on its hind legs with its fore hoofs on Officer Fred's chest, the pig is almost as tall as Fred and probably twice his weight—and Fred's a big boy.

Pod thinks hard for a minute or two. It's hard to think with all that snorting and grunting, most of it coming out of Fred. He'd jump into the fray to assist the officers, but at the moment there is no obvious handhold.

Along comes the Neighbor, also known as Popple, in his Humvee. Popple and Mrs. Popple, new in town, live at the top of the steep knob known as Hosshead Hill so they need four-wheel-drive. They think they do anyway. Naturally, the Neighbor pulls over. The pig is down. Officer Fred's on top. Chief Harold's on the bottom. It's a pig sandwich. Most of the squealing seems to be emanating from Chief Harold.

"Do you know how to control a pig?" Officer Fred asks Popple. Judging from the blank expression on the man's face, he don't.

The Reverend Mr. Claus Titbaum roars up in the muffler-deprived church van; locals call it the Titmobile. No doubt coming from or on his way to an errand of mercy, naturally, he pulls over and inquires whether all is well.

All will be well as soon as the pig is subdued. It is a lively pig.

"Do you know how to control a pig, Father?" Popple asks.

Pod didn't realize the Neighbor and the Reverend Mr. Claus Titbaum were related.

"I'm not a father," The Reverend Mr. Claus Titbaum says, "although I try to be a brother to all."

Meanwhile, Officer Fred and Chief Harold have wrestled the pig away from the big rock—or the pig has wrestled them—and they're rolling down a grassy incline toward the river. Picking up speed as they go. For a minute it looks like they're going to roll into the river. But no. They wedge up against a stump overgrown with what looks a lot like poison ivy. Do you suppose poison ivy affects pigs the same way it affects people?

With cars parked every which way and the lights of the cruiser flashing in his eyes, it's hard for Perley to get through with his 1935 ton-and-a-half Ford dump truck with the flathead V-8. He parks it in the middle of the road, leaves it running. He doesn't like to shut it off, because sometimes it don't like to start up again. "What's going on here?" Perley says. "Is it a convention? Or a riot?"

Officer Fred has the pig in a neck lock. Chief Harold has the pig in a haunch lock. Still, the pig appears to have the advantage.

"Perley," yells Officer Fred. "Do you know how to control a pig?"

"You're doing good, Fred," Perley says. "Keep it up. I think I'll run home and get a camera."

But before Perley manages the high-step into his truck, he's just about run over by Young Barker speeding through on his bicycle on his way home for supper after a ball game. He skids to a stop. Perley says, "Young Barker, do you know how to control a pig?"

"No," Young Barker says, "but my mother does."

That evening at the Barker house, the folks hear the story of the pig and the traffic jam on Flutter Street. "That's amazing," Grammie Barker says, passing the peas. "All that excitement just down the road and the pig finally returned to its pen."

"That's not the amazing part," Young Barker's mother says. "What's amazing is how many people around Flutter Street, including a son of mine, don't know how to control a pig." ✦

A SHORT QUIZ
  (1) How Do You Control a Pig?
  (2) What Was the Pig's Name?
    Answers on page 85.

# *Moosilaukee*

"IT WEREN'T FAR from here," Linn says, "they found the Injun skull with the beak of a loon struck right through the bone. Injun got too close to that loon nest—two hundred, three hundred years ago, who knows—and it's the last thing that Injun ever done." Each stroke of the old man's paddle is a cut and healing of water that cannot touch his eyes for color or clarity—eyes too big by half for his face—a baby's eyes. "Don't s'pose it done the loon much good either."

Mary shivers with the glide of the lake beneath the canoe's ribs and the chill off the water, just two weeks past ice-out. She has paid this stranger fifteen dollars to paddle her from the public launch at Drumlin nearly half the length of the lake to the Moosilaukee Cliffs. He takes his guide duties seriously. "Loon flies to sea," he says, "stays there two, three years 'til the lake says come home. That loon we see, Mary, may be the great great great great grandchild of the one killed the Injun. May be!"

He angles the paddle and the canoe noses toward shore. Long trip this time of year to the Moosilaukee Cliffs. Stick close, stay in the shallows: lake may seem calm as can be, but get caught in the broads, along comes a swamping wave: "Ice water," he says. "You'd think so! Don't worry about drowning, Mary, worry about freezing to death."

Her face is a beautiful mask. She draws up her knees and folds her arms around them. Her long, bright hair falls forward. The tips of her red canvas shoes touch the ribs of the canoe.

"So cold it's not—after just a short while." He studies her face for ripples that might betray the current just under the surface, but she gives no visible sign, this quiet young woman. "By God, Mary, there's worse ways to go!" He reaches for the thermos, the sudden shift of weight tilting the canoe. Mary gasps. For a moment the water surges close, and she's falling into lake shadows. Then the weight shifts again, the world rights, and the canoe is on keel.

"Want some?" he says, and pours into the mug. "It's hot. Warm your bones." She shakes her head, no thanks. "My bones could stand some warming," he says. Lake cold is penetrating on account of the damp: a spring cold can be worse than January, because you don't expect it and you're wishing it away.

Linn sips his coffee. They drift. The canoe glides over silver ledge, black depths, over Mary's pale face staring back at her as she leans out cautiously. A kingfisher dives. Mary braids her hair. The coffee warms Linn's bones. As soon as Mary's braid is complete, it begins to fall out again. Linn clears his throat and tucks the thermos under the seat. "A *lot* worse ways to go," he says, as though he's been imagining them all along. "Like that young fella last spring went over the cliff and—splat—that was the end of him!"

Mary says: "You were on the water that day. You saw him fall." The innkeeper told her Linn's wasn't the only boat on the lake, but it was nearer the cliffs than the others.

"I saw," Linn says.

In fact, it was one year ago today the young man fell to his death. Linn doesn't realize, but Mary does.

"Too high," he says. "That's the trouble. Them cliffs are too high. Sail off like a bird and it feels forever and there's time—that's the trouble. Time to hope for a soft landing. Time to pray, if you're inclined. Time to know there aren't gonna be no soft landing." Not at the foot of the Moosilaukee Cliffs with that fringe of scrub pine to skewer you, and the boulders (no give to them big fellas), a strip of shale beach hard as cement, then the lake. "The trees'll break your fall all right," he says, "and break you, too."

Mary says: "I knew him—the one who fell."

Linn says: "I thought maybe." He'd been wondering what possessed her, why she'd come to him so determined to get out on the lake in the chill and wet crack of dawn on this particular gray day. "Weren't the first," he says, "nor the last." The Moosilaukee cliffs are Injun sacred, so Linn believes, both blessed and cursed, and he should know, descended from Abenaki on one side, Penacook on the other.

Mary says: "I hadn't known him long."

"Long enough, I guess." Linn looks away, because it hurts to look straight at her, like looking into the sun even when it's just a round glow through cloud cover, especially then. At the funeral, after the others had gone, she lay a sprig of lilac among the roses. She didn't go back to the house with his family, friends, colleagues. She didn't want to intrude. Or set them wondering, when there was nothing left to wonder about.

"Don't take so long as you'd think," Linn says. Now he's speaking of the contours of the lake and the distance they must travel to reach the cliffs. "Once you poke through the neck, lake opens up like a fan and you see everything. You will when the fog clears. Don't worry, Mary. It's burning off quick."

She's not worried, she tells him. It's all the same to her: fog or clear, gray or sun, cold or hot, rain or shine. "That's some coincidence," he says, "since I had the same attitude all my life." Don't matter. Shouldn't matter! Wait for the perfect day, and you wait too long, and most people wouldn't recognize one if they were drowning in it.

"They're all perfect days on Moosilaukee," he says. "May be!" Come a downpour, the rest run like cats for cover, but Old Linn's dancing on the dock, more or less. His is a strange little dance and he knows it. A strange little crippled-man's jig. People see it—they don't know whether to laugh or look away.

He rests the paddle and with two fingers demonstrates the jig on his knee. "Pull on my slicker," he says, "Don't matter how fast the rain comes—I'm all set!"

He slaps his knee, tugs at his pant leg, lifts the twisted foot and lets it thunk the floor of the canoe. "You'd be amazed," he says, "I amaze myself!"

On those rare days when rain falls so hard it pocks the lake all over, if you listen close it's like a thousand fingers pounding a thousand keys. "Moosilaukee is music then," he says. "And the music is so . . . if I told you, you'd call me a liar, Mary. Yes you would!"

"I wouldn't," she says. "I'd believe you."

Now he sees the ripples softening her face. Now he is certain the

81

current runs deep. For a young woman she is too old. *Older than me*, Linn thinks. But he is a child in a grown-old body. Never pretended or cared to be anything but.

"Tell me this," Mary says: "When the one who fell, the man who fell, when he was falling, did he cry out?"

Linn studies the lacings on his boots and shakes his head. If she wants to take that as an answer, she's welcome to it, but he will not say more. Not now. He studies the near shore where the lake stretches into wetland. Not a hundred yards away, the shape of a moose separates itself from low-lying mist. He is not surprised by the moose; these woods are thick with them. Still, his breath catches and his gimpy heart skips, because to see a moose is a miracle, even if you've seen a hundred, even if you've seen a thousand over ten lifetimes: the real thing, the living animal before-your-eyes, so much bigger, shaggier, darker, quieter than remembered or imagined. Some say Quiet as a mouse; Linn says, Quiet as a moose.

"See there, Mary," he whispers. "Just turn your head slow."

To its hips in the water, the moose dips and brings up a beard of weeds. Linn lets the paddle drag. As the canoe glides by, the moose grazes undisturbed, though one rolling eye seems to follow them. Mary spots the moose and holds her breath, afraid if she breathes the creature will spook, afraid if she blinks it will disappear. It is her first moose.

She blinks; it disappears. She begins to cry. The tears fall silent and coat her face. She's staring at Linn the way earlier she stared into the water, as though looking for something in particular. Something she needs to see, but is pretty sure she won't. She imagines her reflection in his too-big, too-bright eyes and wonders what he sees. But Linn doesn't see her at all. He's seeing the young man as he falls, the yellow of his jacket against the gray of the cliffs. Linn is remembering how the young man screamed all the way down. Those screams are a secret Linn will keep. They are true. They are also sacred. Even a fool wouldn't inflict such a truth on this sad Mary, and Linn is no fool. "I heard nothing," he says. "Not a bless-ed sound."

"Then how?" she says. She does not raise a hand or a sleeve to wipe the tears. They fall easily. He pictures the tabletop ledge in Cascade Stream, and how the timeless flow of water has worn it smooth as Mary's forehead. Wisps of her hair cling to her cheeks and chin and neck. Her hands clench in her lap. "How did you know to look there, to look up?"

It was the jacket. The bright jacket, at first a speck moving on the trail, then off the trail and along the edge. The young man had to climb over chain strung between iron pipes years ago by the CCC. He had to pass the weathered sign that said: Danger.

Then the surprise of motion, paintbrush yellow across the cliff face. "It was the color caught my eye," he says.

Mary nods. Grateful. She hadn't known the young man long, but he had been tender with her. He had treated her as tenderly as the mosses and rock flowers he collected, rarest of the rare. He had invited her to Moosilaukee to hike with him, to sleep with him under stars, but she'd said no, not yet. Not yet.

"Once he started to go," Linn says, "there was nothing he could do, and nothing to be done, Mary, once that rock give way. Believe me."

They pass through the neck, and, as promised, the lake opens up. It is the biggest inland body of water she has ever seen. The far shore is almost invisible, a gray line, a misty horizon. And she can see for herself, even across the broads, that no one could fall from the Moosilaukee Cliffs and survive. "How could I not believe you?" she says.

A thousand paddle strokes later, like a halved apple—half above water, half below—the Moosilaukee Cliffs rise before them. At first the rock seems to cut straight into the water, straight into itself— the water so still, the light reflecting. But as the canoe skims closer, Mary distinguishes the shale beach, the boulders, the fringe of trees that wraps the base of the sheer stone like a scarf. Some days the lake seems to swallow the cliffs, but today, they are definitely rising. They rise out of their own perfect reflection, their height doubled. She looks up and up. She looks down and down.

Linn says: "This fella asks me, 'How them cliffs get so damn high?' 'Don't know,' I says, 'They were like that when I got here.'" He maneuvers the canoe along the curve of the shore, lapped by their small wake: "Some say glacier. Some say a earthquake split the mountain down the middle and half fell in."

The cliffs approach vertical, but roughly. They are pitted with cracks and shelves and crevices, shallow caves. "Some say it was a strike of lightning hit just right on the fault line. See there!" Linn says. Slicing the face, corner to corner, a bolt of quartz.

"A hundred ninety feet at the height," he says. "But today they look bigger, don't they. Some days I swear they touch the sky."

Mary closes her eyes, but her lids are too thin and the image of the cliffs bleeds through. She can see him falling. She can trace his exact path. In her dreams he is saved. She saves him. They fall and reach for each other and are saved, floating to the water which welcomes them softly. In other dreams she is the one who falls. She falls and falls and wakes up screaming.

She opens her eyes: cliff and sky above and below. She is caught between two worlds, but which way is up? Which is down?

Which is water? Which is air?

Which is grief? Which is hope?

Which is real? Which is reflection?

Is she floating or falling?

Linn sings, "Mary!"—his paddle raised mid-stroke. She focuses on his too-big eyes, on his gentled old man face, and she knows. She reaches for what is real. The canoe tips but not dangerously. The water is cold on her fingertips. She brings her hand to her face. The water is cold on her face. She washes her face with a splash of winter. Wake up, Mary. Wake up, now.

Linn says, "Before I die, there's just one thing I haven't done that I want to—that I wanted to ever since I thought of it about forty years ago."

"Climb to the top?"

But he says, no, nothing drastic like that. The legs he was born with kept him looking up all these years, no need or desire to change that at this late date. "Moose swim in this lake," he says. "Don't know why. Don't know where they think they're going. But I've seen it. Away out in the middle of the lake, you see something real big and real dark—almost black—moving along at a good clip, tracing a wake. Big old homely head and antlers rising out of the water. Bony old moose back slicking along. And down below, bony old moose legs flailing saucer hoofs. Crush a man with those hoofs if it wanted to. But not in the water. Water slows them down and nowhere to run even if they could, which they can't. That's why it's against the law to shoot a moose unless it's on dry land.

"A man in a canoe, paddling brisk, could glide up behind a swimming moose, glide alongside, close enough to look straight into that big old moose's rolling eye and declare his intention. Before I die, I'm going to do it, Mary!" Linn says. "I'm going to paddle alongside, ease myself out of this canoe, and straddle that moose's back. I'm going to hang on tight for dear life. And I'm going to ride that moose, Mary, all the way to shore!" ℘

(1) How Do You Control a Pig?

To control a pig, as Young Barker's mother well knows, you put a bucket on its head and grab its tail. This enables a person to steer the pig, because if a pig can't see where it's going, it is open to suggestion.

(2) What Was the Pig's Name?

Destiny.

Funny name for a pig.

# SURVIVING WINTER

*Driving out across Big Lake in Alan's Dodge Dakota, going fishing after the freeze, Pod asked about the plastic milk jug tied on a long rope dragging the ice behind them.*

*"Oh," Alan says. "That's so if we go through, they'll know where to find us."* ❧

*The cousin from the city wanted to know what folks did in New Hampshire all winter.*

*"Oh," the native said, "Mostly, we start cars."* ❧

*Wouldn't you know, coldest day of the year and the toilet stops working. Royal can't figure out what the problem is, so he bites the bullet and calls in Joe the Plumber. Joe arrives at the door, tool kit in hand.*

*"The bathroom's right through there," Royal says. "Go on in, but pull the door tight shut behind you. Mother's taking a tub and if there's a draft, she'll be ugly."* ❧

*At the Paisley Town Meeting, the issue of buying a new snowplow came up on the warrant. Spirited discussion ensued. Why couldn't they fix the old plow? Had they put the thing out for bids? Why'd they have to go and buy a Cadillac of plows when, truth be told, this was a Volkswagen town? Maybe next year, but not this year. This year people's wallets were stretched to the limit. How are the old people supposed to live? Etc.*

*Finally, Pod came up with an idea. He says: "I heard from my Uncle*

87

*Perley they got a snowplow on the warrant down to Woodford, also.
Why can't we go in with them and split the cost?"*

*Judy Fineswold, the Road Agent, couldn't let that comment pass. She
says, "Jesum, Pod, as far as I know, when it's snowing in Paisley it's
snowing in Woodford, too."* ❧

# Skivvies

YES, IT WAS a cold winter. No question about it. But there've been
colder. Royal remembered his Grampa John telling about one in
particular.

Ezra says: "That wa'n't the winter the town clock froze, was it,
Royal?"

"I believe it was. It could have been. It got so cold with the snow
and sleet freezing on the town clock, it stopped. And they didn't get
it going again until spring."

"Hard winters back then," Ezra says. "Not like now, these warm
piddly things they call winter. A lot of days I don't even bother to
light the stove. And the piddly little bit of snow that piddles down,
hardly enough to bother with. Wait for spring. Let it melt."

Ezra is known to be warm blooded.

Urban says: "Cold weather don't phase Ezra. New Year's day last
year I happened to drive by his place. Don't know where I was going, but I must have been going somewhere. It was a nippy day—20,
30 below—but the sun was out. There sat Ezra in his swim trunks.
I guess it was his swim trunks, either that or his skivvies, stretched
out like a mud worm on the front porch. Getting a tan."

"Is that right?" Royal says.

"I guess it must be," Ezra says. "Urban don't lie. Neither of course
does his brother, Nelson. Neither of course do the politicians down
to Concord."

Royal says: "I never seen Ezra wearing anything but his overalls
and undershirt—summer, winter, spring, or fall. I figured that was
your uniform, Ezra. Must have been quite a sight, 30 below and

Ezra stretched out like a mud worm in his swim trunks. Or was it his skivvies?"

"I don't know," Urban says, "but it wa'n't pretty." ♪

# The Sled

ROYAL SAYS: "DID your grampa ever tell you about the most amazing object ever sighted in the town of Wakefield?"

Urban says: "Don't get going on them UFOs again, Royal. Alma'll have you put away, you keep that up."

Joey says: "Is it the gigantic pike you caught when you were little?"

Royal says no: "That's the second most amazing thing. The first most amazing thing was Mr. Pearl's sled, the biggest double-runner sled in the world and also the fastest because the more people you put on a sled, the faster it goes. You put one person on a sled going down a steep hill and it goes pretty fast. You put on two or three or four, it's whizzing. You put on a hundred, you're flying."

Joey says: "Grampa and I go really fast on my sled. Don't we, Grampa?"

Ezra says: "We get up a good head of steam on the hard-pack."

Royal says: "You could put a hundred people or more on Mr. Pearl's sled because it was 78 feet long. Loaded and with the snow just right, it could get going so fast that when the one in front screamed, the one in back never heard it. The sled was going faster than the scream. Now, that's fast."

Joey says: "I bet you were scared."

Royal says: "No. Hardly. Well, a little. The one steering had to pay right attention, that's for sure. One time I got elected to steer and had a lapse. I guess I had a lapse, because the next thing I knew, instead of going downhill, we were sluicing up a knob—"

Joey says: "Did you have an accident? Did the hundred people fall off?"

Royal says: "Thinking quick, I yelled, 'Lean back,' and everybody leaned back. It pulled up the nose of that sled so the knob acted kinda like a ski jump and the whole business went airborne.

"Started out in Union. Landed in Milton. And skidded almost into downtown Rochester before we brung the thing to a complete stop.

"Luckily, in those days, Joey, there wa'n't much traffic." ⅌

# Bub Goes to a Card Party

BUB DIDN'T EVEN know L.E. had a sister until the day she delivered sandwiches to the mill. The water rushed through the sluice gate and the saws whirred and whirled, so she stood on the ledge that jutted into the pond and waved the lunch bag to get L.E.'s attention.

She got Bub's.

Afterwards, when a load of scraps needed delivering to the farm on Ford Hill, Bub volunteered to drive the wagon. He'd wave to Mother on the porch shelling peas or Julia weeding the kitchen garden. Call out to Old Man Ford, "Where you want these scraps dumped?"

"Scrap pile seems a goddamn likely spot, don't it?"

Bub and Old Man got along fine. As for Bub and Julia: "Does she have a steady fella," he asked L.E. kind of casual.

L.E. pulled his short black pipe out of his mouth, his trademark, and reached into the bib of his overalls for his tobacco pouch. "Steady stream of them up the house," he said. "Can't tell one from the other."

Bub was hopeful.

One Saturday night, deep winter, the East Avery cousins were invited to play Crazy Eights for pennies and L.E. invited Bub, too. After work, he snowshoed the mile or so up the hill to the farm. In those days the roads weren't plowed. If the snow got deep, they rolled them.

Bub lost at Crazy Eights, which was the right thing to do. He seemed to be making headway. Nobody got to fighting anyway, which was good; the hard cider mellowed everybody out pretty much. Bub was feeling real mellow when, at the end of the evening, Old Man yawned, Mother handed Bub his hat, and L.E. said, "I can save you some time, Bub, and ski you down over the hill."

The East Woodford cousins had already left. L.E. was to retrieve their horse and sleigh at the mill and bring it back to the farm where it was needed for church in the morning. "We've got just the one pair of skis," L.E. said, "but it's a good smooth ride down over."

Julia showed some concern: "I don't recommend it," she said. But Old Man thought it was a great idea. And Mother just put her hands over her eyes.

"It's a fine moonlight night," L.E. said. Which it was. The moon was full. Snow ghosts clung to the tree trunks and branches, draped the stone walls. Bub and L.E. bundled up. Bub strapped on his pack and the bear-paw snowshoes over it.

The skis were seven feet long and six inches wide. Plenty of room for L.E.'s big feet to buckle on, but there was just the one set of buckles. No buckles for Bub. He lined up behind L.E. and muckled onto his waist. "Bend your knees when I do," L.E. said. "Curl your toes so you don't slide off."

The lucky thing was there were wagon wheel ruts iced into the road. On the far right were two clean cut ruts, strategically placed about a foot and a half apart. L.E. said they could ride those ruts all the way to the bottom; he wouldn't even have to steer.

"All right," Bub said. "I'm ready!"

Julia, Mother, and Old Man waved them off. Julia said, "Now you be careful," which made Bub smile. L.E. lit his pipe, inserted it, raised his long bamboo pole in salute. Bub didn't get any poles.

The slope started out gradual. L.E.'s smoke blew around them like a cloud. The moon was so bright that by looking over L.E.'s shoulder, Bub could see quite a ways ahead. *Hey*, he thought, *this ain't so bad.* Steady over the bumps, anticipating the curves, leaning one way or the other. It had taken almost an hour to snowshoe up the hill earlier that evening; they'd ski down in minutes.

Their moon shadows slid over the snowy stone walls: one tall with pipe and poles; the other not-so tall with a stocking cap streaming behind. They picked up speed. Bub's eyes stung from the wind.

They negotiated a long curve with considerable grace. Bub began to feel cocky. Confident. Almost invincible. They approached a long steep open grade, the steepest part of the whole ride. They sped through the night.

Everything was going along smooth until, at the edge of Bub's vision, as far ahead as he could see by squinting, he spotted a black lump against the ghostly white snow. L.E. spotted it, too, at about the same time.

The lump got bigger.

And bigger.

It seemed to fill their left rut.

Thinking quick, L.E. said, "Bub, we're going to have to lift our left feet."

Bub could see he was right. The black lump that filled their left rut was a large, frozen horse-flap.

They lifted their left feet.

But something went wrong. Some slight miscalculation. L.E. went one way. Bub went the other. They tipped end-over-end, ass over teakettle. Poles, pack, snowshoes took flight. L.E. tucked into a ball and rolled. Bub flipped, slid, somersaulted, and landed face first with a snowshoe on his head. It was surprisingly comfortable sprawled there in the snow. Comfortable and comforting to be breathing and in no particular pain. He thought he'd lay still and rest. Also, he was a dite worried about trying to move any of his extremities, worried they might not do what it was he asked them to.

After awhile, could have been a minute, could have been a week, he heard a hoarse voice close to but muffled by the snow in his ears, "Bub," the voice said. "I've lost my pipe."

And so the night's adventure became a story. Some said one of the skis slid on its own clear to the village, but that's a lie. Some said L.E. and Bub tumbled all the way to the mill and wedged up against the slab pile, but that's an exaggeration. Some said L.E.'s pipe didn't turn up until spring when Mother, out picking strawberries, spied it in the field, none the worse for wear, which is mainly true. Some said L.E. and Bub bounced like India rubber and, though achy for a day or two, came out of it like the pipe, none the worse for wear, which is a matter of opinion, as Bub's tailbone reminds him now and then. Folks agreed on one thing: Bub was accepted into the family that night, which must be so, because less than a year later, he and the beautiful Julia tied the knot. And that, my friend, is a fact. ✒

# Thin Ice

THOSE EARLY WINTER evenings, Monty was at the sewing machine by the window, sock foot, pumping the treadle. The cabin was dark except for the round light from a gooseneck lamp illuminating the fabric as he fed it under the needle. So far as he knew, he and the woman in the cedar-shake house across the lake were the only ones around for miles. When the sun set, the shoreline went black, except for the yellow light that poured from her windows and reflected off the water, like eyes looking at eyes.

With binoculars he could distinguish her figure, not details, but the general shape of her—seated, bending, reaching, moving. She seemed often to be moving. A busy woman, purposeful. At night, when her light went out, he sometimes stood on the porch in the cold, listening, breathing, sensing the space over the water, sensing but not seeing the densely-tree'd horizon until his eyes adjusted to starlight or moonlight, if there were any.

He wondered if maybe, in that intense darkness, she stood at her window or on her porch, looking at his window, his light, until it too blinked out. After a while he stopped using the binoculars, because of an inkling that if he kept it up, some time soon when he adjusted the focus he might catch her looking at him through binoculars of her own.

During the day, when he and the dog were out tinkering on the snowmobile, piling stone into wall, splitting wood, gathering kindling, he'd spot her outside, too—a silhouette between the house and the outbuildings, or walking the beach between her place and the point. If the dog noticed her, he'd bark. "She's not bothering anybody, Jules," Monty would say. "Pipe down, now." Jules, generally, kept barking until the woman moved out of sight, or Monty dragged him into the cabin. Sometimes, even that wasn't enough to quiet him. "Come on!" Monty might say. "You're hurting my head." If he spoke too harshly, Jules would hunker down. He'd roll on his back, legs stretched, belly exposed, as if to say: "Sorry."

Then Monty would feel sorry, too.

His ex-wife Sue noticed right away he was as low as he had ever been. "Why do you want to go and spend the winter in the boondocks?" she said. "No need of it, Monty. John and I'll put you up."

"I'm all right," he said. "The dog and I are doing just fine." He tapped his chest over the heart, as though that were the source of the lie (which maybe it was) and grinned.

When the dog laid his big head on his boot, Monty bent to scratch the soft, flat ears. He raked the thick coat at the dog's shoulders, down the length of his back.

"He's drooling," Sue said. "That's fairly gross."

"He's happy." Monty lifted the dog's chin. "He's smiling. See? Like me."

"Snow comes," she said, "you'll be stuck out here through mud season."

"No problem. Nowhere to go. That's the beauty part."

By spring, he'd have his license back. By spring, some job would open up—on the state roads, at the campground, in the lumber yard. Some job he'd had before or a cousin to it. And he'd be back in the thick of what passed for making a living and living a life. Probably.

"If you're going to be unemployed," she said, "you might as well keep busy." Homemade quilts sold like hotcakes at the shop. The summer people didn't care if the quilts were fancy, so long as they were cotton and under a hundred bucks. Besides groceries, on her second visit Sue hauled in fabric, quilt books, and a treadle sewing machine. "I'd let you borrow my electric," she said, "but you might hurt yourself."

Monty liked the rhythm of the foot pedal and the thum-thum-thum of the needle, especially when he sewed the top to the stuffing and backing—three layers so thick the needle would break unless he kept the material taut, easing the stitches one by one.

The first quilt he finished—a log cabin—was so homely, he threw it down for the dog, who pawed it into a heap. "It's O.K., Jules," Monty said. "It's for you."

The dog sighed, settled, his head lolling on his paws. "Enjoy it," Monty said.

Jules did.

"Not exactly a work of art," Sue said when she saw the quilt and Jules on it. "You sewed it crooked for one thing. And the colors . . . not a combination I would have picked."

"The dog likes it."

"Of course he does," she said. "It might not be pretty, but it's soft; it's warm. Right, Jules?"

The dog lifted his head and pressed his nose into her palm. "You're a good boy," she said. "You're just a big sweet lovey guy," which was pretty much the same thing she'd said to Monty twenty-odd years ago. "You're a good guy, Monty; you're just a big sweet lovey guy . . ." They'd had to get married, she said, but they didn't have to stay married now that there was no baby in the picture. "We want different things," she said—which had been news to him.

He grinned, for godsakes, the day they signed the papers. Been grinning ever since. Pretty much.

For Monty's second quilt, Sue picked the pattern—trip-around-the-world. She also chose the colors and wrote down their order. This time he should concentrate on cutting straight, sewing straight. "It's not hard," she said. "But you've got to pay attention, Monty."

"Measure once, cut twice," he said.

"Something like that."

It had been a strange, empty winter so far—if you could call it winter. Not much snow, not much cold, not much of anything. Nights, when the temperature dropped, the lake would skim with grease ice. Then the sun would rise, the breeze would pick up, holes would open around the rocks and the islands. Noon time, the ice was pretty much gone, the water black and choppy.

By January, Monty and Jules were both sick of quilts, sick of looking at the cabin walls (they'd memorized every knothole), sick of not fishing because the ice was too thin, sick of not snowmobiling because there was no snow to speak of either.

One entertaining thing: most days an otter would appear on a rock between Monty's place and the point. He'd pop up through water that never seemed to freeze even when the skim ice all around turned white and seemed likely to stay—something about the way the sun hit that particular spot, or the current, or the upwelling of a spring. Maybe it was the activity of the otter itself that scared the ice away.

When it appeared, preening and rolling as if it were joyously alone in the world, Jules would growl in his throat, hum a while near his back teeth, and, eventually, whine in frustration, or longing. "What's he think he's doing out there, Jules?" Monty would say. "What's that little fella up to?"

The otter might stay five minutes or an hour—depending, Monty supposed, on what else he had going that day. But the whole time, Jules would stare and hum and whine. Through the binoculars, Monty could see the sheen of the animal's fur, the curve of its back, the mystery of its wild eye.

Might have been the otter who lured the dog onto the ice. Maybe Jules spotted it on the rock, *again*, and couldn't stand it. Maybe he had to make contact: sniff it, chase it, bite it, eat it, something! Maybe the dog was on the ice and a good distance from shore before it dawned on him that although the lake was bottled over, it groaned under his weight, and thundered a warning—*go back*— more vibration than sound. Maybe that's why when he reached the middle, he flattened out and didn't move for a long time.

Long enough for Monty to spot him and yell, "Jules! Get your furry butt back here!" Long enough for the woman across the lake to spot him. When she yelled, the dog must have thought it was an invitation, because he raised himself up and loped in her direction.

That's when the ice gave out.

All around him, it seemed to soften, dissolve, as though he'd only imagined it, as though he'd been walking on water all along. Which he had, pretty much. All at once, he was under, seeking air, then scrambling for a toe hold. But the more he clawed and heaved, the more water there seemed to be.

"Jules! You stupid dog." Monty was running. Maybe if he ran fast enough, the ice would break behind him instead of beneath him. He ran as fast as he could with a rake in his arms, a coil of rope over his shoulder, a blue plastic sled flopping behind. He ran as fast as when he'd run track in high school, not fast enough to win, but fast enough to impress Sue—to catch her eye and her heart, briefly.

*This may be the stupidest thing I've ever done*, Monty thought, but kept on running, because nothing could live long in that cold, cold water. When he got close, close enough, he slowed, paused, stood and pondered: Should he knot the rope and toss it? Tie up the rake and toss that? Should he ease himself forward, belly down on the blue sled? He considered his choices for about five heart beats. Then the ice decided it had had enough of Monty, too.

Down he went.

He felt the heat sucked from his body, all at once. Then, it wasn't cold anymore—or if it was, he couldn't tell. Couldn't feel a thing. But his arms still moved, and his legs. His brain told them to move—time passed—they moved. He used the blue sled's buoyancy to float toward Jules. The lake made room.

The tip of the dog's nose was above water, his eyes. Monty grabbed the collar. *That last quilt was a good one*, he thought, *but I'm never going to finish it*. He wondered why his life wasn't passing before his eyes—or maybe it just had.

Then somebody was there with him, cracking the ice around him, yelling: "Grab hold!"

"Hold of what?" Monty said.

The woman from across the lake poked the spoon end of a paddle in Monty's direction. She'd poled the canoe over the ice and into the open water. She and it were floating beside him—close enough to touch, almost.

She reached for him. "Come on," she said, "grab hold, get in."

Monty lifted the dog by the collar, dead weight, tried to slide the blade of the paddle under him.

"The rope," she said.

He knew the rope was somewhere, but couldn't locate it.

"Raise your arm," she said. "Sling it over the side."

He knew he had an arm, but couldn't locate it.

She leaned. The canoe leaned, too. She found his arm for him, grabbed the rope, wrapped it twice around his wrist, twice around the cross bracing.

He raised Jules' soggy head, levered the dog high as he could with the paddle, maneuvered him over the rise of the gunnel, thud, into the bottom of the canoe.

"Ready?" she said. Didn't wait for an answer. She was paddling hard and deep. Her weight and the weight of the dog lowered the keel and raised the bow, so when they hit the shelf, the whole business sluiced out of the water and on to good ice, Monty dragging behind like a trout on a stringer.

Near shore, he rolled around to make sure he wasn't frozen stiff, crawled to the canoe and propped himself up to look in. The dog's eyes were open, gleaming, but he wasn't moving. The dog had nothing to say. The woman said, "How you doing?"

Monty said, "Been better."

In the cedar-shake house, she dried them off, wrapped them up, poured hot tea down Monty's gullet, and threatened to call the rescue squad. "We're all right," Monty said. Jules was sneezing, shaking, beginning to show signs of life. "We'll be all right."

"It'll be a wonder if you don't catch pneumonia."

Jules dragged himself onto the couch beside Monty, who said: "You're getting the nice lady's quilt all wet. What ails you?" But Jules was already poking the quilt into a heap, settling. Monty recognized the quilt pattern from a book Sue gave him: the navy curves fanning over white, almost but not quite interlocking. "Drunkard's Path," he said, and grinned.

"No," she said. "The one who made it gets to name it. I call it Birds of a Feather."

She was not as young as he thought she'd be. Nor as old. She was not as pretty, nor as homely either. Her face was neither smooth, nor particularly lined. Her eyes wondered, kindly. "It's not just shapes," she said. "See the wings, the tails, the beaks?"

"Birds?"

"I'm an artist," she said. "I notice these things. It's not so much what you're seeing as how you see it."

He saw an easel and on it a painting of the view from the window: white ice, the otter, the rock, his cabin hulking across the way. "You're good."

"No," she said, "I'm not. That's the problem."

"No," he said. "You are."

She didn't argue. She accepted the gift of his admiration with a nod and a hint of a blush—or was it chap from the cold?

Monty looked again at the quilt she had made, more closely this time—the tiny stitches, the perfect corners, the duplicate curves, the contrast of light and dark. He curved one hand over Jules' damp head. With the other, he traced the shape of one bird in flight, then another. ❧

# CHRISTMAS

*At the end of Christmas dinner, everyone tucked into apple pie. After one bite, Mother said: "Oh, I'm sorry, this isn't as good as I usually make."*

*Daughter-in-law snapped, "I made that one."* ❧

*For the holidays, Doris, a kindergarten teacher, liked to make sugar cookies and put them in tins for the neighbors. One Christmas, she said, a mistake was made. She had a bowl of cookie batter, cheery green, chilling in the fridge, and a bowl of homemade playdough—also cheery green.*

*The bowls got switched and she didn't realize until she'd given away several tins of playdough cookies. She felt terrible . . . until a neighbor called and asked for the recipe.* ❧

## Mavis Goes to Yoga: A Christmas Story

### Part I

MAVIS WON A certificate for "Introduction to Yoga: Embrace the Earth" in the Fine Pine Social Club Raffle at the Woodford Holiday Craft Extravaganza and Bake Sale. She had her eye on the light-up plastic elf (which looked something like her husband, Perley), but somebody from out-of-town won him. Isn't that always the way?

It was a shame, too. The elf had a pointy hat and ears, rosy cheeks, shoes that curled at the ends. If you pushed a button on his back, he said: "Which way to the North Pole?" Would have looked real cute on the roof with the plywood sleigh and reindeer, which, as a matter-of-fact, Perley and the neighbor were in the process of hoisting into place this chill, blustery morning.

Which was why Mavis had wanted to get out of the house. Perley on the roof made her nervous, especially when the wind tried to sail that sleigh like a kite, even with the neighbor steadying the ladder and yelling up instructions, "Back a dite; no, it's crooked. Too far, Perley."

It was a nerve-wracking business as far as Mavis was concerned. She said prop it up in the side yard and call it good. But Perley said: "The prancing and pawing of each little *hoof.* On the *roof.*"

Mavis didn't even know what yoga was exactly, except it maybe involved standing on your head or sitting pretzel-legged and staring off into space—none of which appealed to her.

"Susie does yoga," Gert said. "She really enjoys it." Susie was Gert's middle daughter, a dental hygienist and marathoner. "Says it takes her to a 'serene place'."

If Mavis wanted to go to a serene place, she'd take a nap. Actually, any time Perley was out of the house seemed serene by comparison. Since he retired, he'd been keeping himself occupied—carving bowls out of burls, painting things, growing tomatoes in the bathroom. In his spare time he was braiding a rug.

"How big is that rug going to be, Perley?" Mavis asked.

"Big," he said.

"Where are you going to put it?"

"Living room."

"It's already too big for the living room."

"Not if I knock out that far wall."

At the crafts table, Mavis picked out a Santa shaped potholder. His beard was sheeting strips. Trouble was if you set Santa too close to the burner, that beard might catch.

"Going to buy it?" Gert said.

Mavis shook her head. "Too hairy," then happened to think maybe the lady behind the table crafted it. *Fox pox,* Mavis thought, yankee for *faux pas.*

Gert said: "I wouldn't mind taking that certificate off your hands. Just so it doesn't go to waste. Somehow, Mavis, I don't think you're the yoga type." And she laughed; let go with a hee-haw that turned heads all over the gym. You could see the question on startled faces: "Where is that noise coming from?" It was coming from Gert.

"How do you know I'm not the yoga type?" Mavis said. "Maybe I am the yoga type. I could be."

## *Part II*

"Assume the corpse position." The instructor demonstrated by lying flat on her back, arms at her sides, palms up.

"Lay down, Mavis," said Gert, who had paid to be in this class and Mavis knew why: so she could report back on Mavis's progress or lack of it. "Assume the corpse position. Don't just sit there."

Earlier, Perley had dropped the two of them off. Said he had to drive into town anyway, stop in at Handy Hardware and buy a chimney brush because his old one, Big Scratchy, had disintegrated. "I hope you're not planning to clean that chimney today," Mavis said. "Don't you dare set foot on the roof until the neighbor gets home to spot you. You'll turn me into a nervous wreck, Perley, prancing around on that roof every ten minutes. What do you think you are, a squirrel?"

"Heights don't bother me," Perley said.

No, they bothered Mavis.

"Let loose the cares of the day. Let them be absorbed by the welcoming earth." Mavis pictured Perley teetering on the peak like a tightrope walker. What if he lost his footing? A fall like that, at his age, he'd be lucky if a leg or an arm was all he broke.

What was the sense of even talking to a man who'd agree to your face, then go ahead and do just as he liked? And when you said something about it later, he'd look blank, "Huh?"

"Feel the tension leave your toes, the arch of your foot, your heels, your ankles, your calves, your knees, your thighs, your hips. Collapse the pelvic girdle . . ." Mavis pulled up short on that one. Gert, too, apparently; she stifled a hee-haw two arm lengths away, fluorescent in fuchsia tights and top with yellow piping. "God help us," Perley had said when Gert arrived at the house that morning all decked out.

"Let your buttocks melt."

Mavis glanced at Gert whose unmelted buttocks raised her off her mat like twin volleyballs.

"Let the warmth spread through your body." Even swathed in sweat shirt, sweat pants and thick socks, Mavis felt no warmth, only the chill of a coming storm through the cement-block walls and slab floor of the Woodford Community Center. And in the narrow window set up high in the cement block wall, snow—the flakes were small, fast falling. It was a storm all right, and a good one, just in time for Christmas.

## *Part III*

Mavis and Gert waited behind the heavy glass doors, watched the nearly empty parking lot fill with snow. "Maybe we should try calling again," Gert said. But they'd already called five times on the pay phone. They'd let it ring and ring.

Just then Chief Harold emerged from town hall and Mavis shouldered open the door. "Chief, is Fred anywhere around, do you know?" Fred was Perley's younger brother and a part-time Woodford police officer.

"On patrol. First snow of the season, you know, and people forget how to drive."

Gert said: "We thought Fred might give Mavis and me a lift. We seem to be stranded."

"I'll give you girls a lift," Chief Harold said. "It's right on the way."

*To where*, Mavis wondered, since they lived on a dead-end. But she didn't say it.

## *Part IV*

Mavis got a bad feeling somewhere in the vicinity of her pelvic girdle when she spotted Perley's pickup in the driveway, quilted in snow. When she slid out of the cruiser, her feet had a hard time finding the ground: the snow so heavy, the sky so white. If it wasn't for gravity you wouldn't know which end was up.

She slogged toward the house and tugged open the door, sweeping a layer of snow from the step with the flat rubber weather seal. "Perley," she called to the empty house, "Perley?"

"Truck's here," Gert said. "Door's unlocked. He's got to be around somewhere."

"Check the roof," Mavis said, though she'd already looked over the part you could see from this side. "Better check out back," she said bleakly.

As they rounded the corner, Gert said, "Wooo," and did a jig. "This stuff is some greasy."

"Don't fall!"

"I have no intention of falling."

Chief Harold stopped in his police-issue rubber tracks by the holly hedge. He stared ahead at an indentation in the snow. *Oh my god*, Mavis thought, *it's Perley, prostrated.*

But the indentation was fifteen-feet long and barred across—the aluminum extension ladder. Chief Harold, Mavis and Gert stepped away from the fallen ladder to view the eastern expanse of roof.

Just below the peak, huddled in the windbreak of the plywood sleigh and reindeer was a pitiful sight.

"God help us," Gert said.

Mavis didn't know what to say.

Well, several comments did cross her mind. Like: "Perley, I told you not to go up on the roof with the neighbor gone and nobody to spot you. And in a snow storm! Can't leave you alone for ten minutes to go off to yoga and learn how to get to a serene place. How am I supposed to get to a serene place the way you act? Are you five? Are you five years old? Because you act about five years old and too damned cheap to pay some young person to get up on the damned roof and clean the damned chimney. Oh no! And I worked real hard this morning to get rid of all my pent-up tension, and now it's back. And it's your fault."

But she didn't say it. She knew what he'd say. He'd say: "I wanted to make a nice surprise for you, Mavis. A Christmas surprise."

And she'd say: "Perley, you promised to stay off the roof."

And he'd say: "Huh?"

Meanwhile, Chief Harold raised the ladder from its snowy resting place to the roof edge.

"I'm going inside," Mavis said. "You can haul him down if you want, Chief, but if it were up to me, I'd leave him." She sent a final blazing glare in the direction of the pitiful sight on the roof—two pitiful sights actually, two snowy lumps whose features were hard to distinguish, but if you looked carefully—even with snow stinging your eyes and melting on your face—you could make out a pointy hat and ears, rosy cheeks, glazed eyes, and the tips of a pair of curled-on-the-end shoes. And beside that lump, one slightly larger with snow coned on a woolly cap, clinging to woolly ear flaps, rosy cheeks, glazed eyes, a drawn-up collar; snow sifted over bent knees, and piled so high around the feet you couldn't tell but maybe that one had curled-on-the-end shoes, too.

Chief Harold climbed to the top of the ladder and looked the situation over. He studied the lump on the right and the lump on the left, then the lump on the right again. He called down to Mavis and Gert. "One of them must be Perley. But, by God, from this angle it's hard to tell which."

Just then, one elf twitched and the snow cascaded around him; one elf spoke. But Mavis was already out of earshot, headed for the door. And she wasn't particularly interested, at that moment, in anything either of them had to say. ❧

# *Christmas Crawlers*

THE TRADITIONAL CHRISTMAS Crawl started after the Great Christmas Disaster of 1962. It insures that such a disaster never recurs, but also it's fun. The Stalwarts try to find fun in all endeavors. When Stacey had to dig through permafrost to the septic tank one Christmas eve, then shimmy down, hoist the pump, and repair the wiring before any Stalwart dared flush the toilet, his twin brother Gerry caught him in a flashlight beam just as he was emerging from the hole. "How's it going?" Gerry said. He would have reached down and lent a hand except Stacey smelled so rank and looked so brown and slippery. "Not bad," Stacey replied. " 'Bout like camping."

The Stalwarts have many traditions that make the holidays special, like the Serving of the Pea. One Christmas, Nana asked if everyone had peas. Hubert responded, "I need a pea," prompting her to spoon one on to his plate. There it lay, beside the cranberry sauce.

This scene has been reenacted year after year. Someone says, "I need a pea" and one pea is placed beside the cranberry sauce, creating a green and red tableau—the colors of the season. It is, inevitably, a poignant moment.

But, getting back to the Disaster and the tradition it inspired. Before anybody gets peas or cranberry sauce, before any food appears on the table, the Christmas Crawl must take place.

Everybody sits—except the previously designated Crawler. Somebody says, "All set?" The Crawler replies: "I'll check," goes under the table, and crawls from one end to the other. The family calls out words of warning and encouragement: "Mind the cross brace." "Keep your head down." "Watch out for Lester's rat." Et cetera.

If you're raised with a tradition, you think nothing much of it. Some families hang stockings by the fireplace; others pin paper bags to the overstuffed chair. Some tag Christmas trees at a farm; others send marksmen deep into Stalwart Swamp to shoot the top off a big old spruce. (They grow back, you know, those tops. Sort of.) If it's your family tradition, it seems normal. Occasionally, when someone imports an in-law, some explanation may be necessary.

"It's like this, Glenn," the Stalwarts explain to the sweet-faced sailor from Georgia that Lucy married. "We Crawl because in 1962 we didn't and, as it turns out, we should have."

That Christmas the family gathered as usual at the homestead on Kettledrum Pond Road. Must have been twenty-two or -three Stalwarts at the sitting. The dining room table was loaded to groaning and stretched to its limit with three oak leafs. The turkey alone went thirty pounds. Uncle Hubert raised it himself.

Hubert Junior says the turkey's name was Big Pecker, but others claim that nickname was something the men made up afterwards to be smart.

Grump was standing over the turkey, which may or may not have been named Big Pecker, a fork in one hand, a carving knife in the other. To the left and right of the turkey, the fixings were abundant: steaming bowls piled high with boiled onions, mashed potatoes, blue hubbard squash. A tureen of peas. Lila's green bean and mushroom soup casserole. Two or three gravy boats filled to the brim. Pitchers of apple cider. A platter of olives, pickles, piccalilli, and dilly beans.

The twenty-two or -three Stalwarts let loose a collective "ooh" of anticipation as Grump sliced into that enormous, juicy bird.

"And then, Glenn, a bad thing happened."

Perley says, "Luckily Mavis and I were setting on the uphill side."

"Not me," Stacey says. "I was downhill and right in front of me, a pail of Aunt Lila's green bean and mushroom soup casserole."

One minute the Stalwarts were drooling over Grump's first cut into that juicy golden monster of a turkey, and the next minute the weight of that holiday dinner became too much for that old dining room table stretched to its limit with three oak leafs.

Once one leg let go it wasn't long before its partner on the downhill side followed suit. Grump stabbed the turkey with the fork, but it was awful heavy and, though the tines were long, they weren't long enough. The turkey escaped and gravity did the rest. The avalanche was swift and inevitable. It involved onions, peas, potato, blue hubbard squash, cranberry sauce, gravy, Lila's green bean and mushroom soup casserole, butter, salt and pepper, olives, pickles, piccalilli and dilly beans. The homemade rolls rolled. The pitchers of apple cider pitched. The downhill Stalwarts were packed so close together between the table and the wall, they could not get out of the way in time. They received that Christmas dinner in their Stalwart laps.

"Isn't it good," Nana said, after a brief, stunned silence, "the pies are still on the sideboard and we saved the hot coffee until dessert?"

And so the tradition of the Christmas Table Crawl was born. When the Crawler emerges at the far end of the table, having checked for weaknesses, especially in the legs, he or she gives the go-ahead. Then and only then is the table loaded with turkey and fixings. Then and only then do the Stalwarts tuck in.

After that, dinner proceeds pretty much without interruption right through until pie, except for the pea discussion and, of course, the apple cider toast, led by the oldest Stalwart present: "Here's to Great Grampa Oliver Stalwart, struck dead from apoplexy as he fished the Mayfly hatch on Kettledrum Pond in Nineteen Sixteen. He got his limit." ❧

# GHOSTS, ETC.

*Back in the 70s, a young man got a good deal on a used hearse. Hey, it ran! He wasn't superstitious. Anyway he went to the Aubuchon Hardware one Saturday morning to rent a sanding machine. The clerk helped him haul it out to the hearse. "Oh," the clerk says, "I see you're smoothing them out some before you plant 'em."* ❧

*Frank was a life-long bachelor who, at the age of 96, married his housekeeper—a young thing in her seventies. Poor Frank died just a year later. At least, they say in town, old Frank died happy.* ❧

*The day after I turned fifty, I was telling stories at a retirement village. I announced to the crowd: "Yesterday I turned fifty." I could see they weren't all that impressed. Thinking quick, I added: "Yup, yesterday I turned fifty. I guess I'm about halfway there."*

*Thinking quicker, a lady piped up: "I'm ninety-nine. Guess I'm about all the way there."* ❧

*At the annual meeting of the Woodford Historical Society, I sat between the town historian and a relative newcomer to town. During dinner we got to talking about cemeteries. (You know how you do.) The newcomer says, "I've been thinking about buying a plot for me and my family."*

*The historian says, "You know, you used to be able to buy a four-body plot for fifteen dollars. These days it'll cost you $1500 or $2000 depending on whether you want the upper or lower cemetery. Course," she added, "you can get scattered for nothing."* ❧

*A New Hampshire native explained that she had lived in Jasper, Georgia, for many years because of work. She got a call from a public servant who asked if she might be interested in buying a plot in a new cemetery they were opening up.*

*"No," she said, "I would not. I already have a plot in Jaffrey, New Hampshire, and I can't wait to get back to it."* ❧

*When Father was on his last legs and his son and daughter-in-law had come home to care for him in his last weeks, the daughter-in-law went to JC Pennys to buy him a flannel shirt, since his were pretty tattered. When the clerk reminded her, "This is a final sale," the daughter-in-law replied: "I know."*

*Later, when the old man had succumbed, she called a local florist about flower arrangements. The florist recommended the "Fireside Bouquet," which the daughter-in-law declined since Father was a God-fearing man, headed, she thought, for heaven and not the other direction.* ❧

# *Jane, My Ghost*

IT IS STILL light outside, barely, the edge of dusk. Through the window over the sink, I see four uniformed police officers in the road, abreast, advancing down the hill. Their breath steams the air. They move slow—alert, wary, as though they are the hunted. One carries a rifle in the crook of her arm. Two hold shotguns across their chests. The fourth walks with his hand on a holster strapped to his hip, cocksure.

I'm married to that one. But not for long.

By the mailbox, they confer. Lester glances toward the house. Maybe he sees me at the window. Maybe not. He gives no sign, but strides up the driveway, onto the porch, and would have marched straight into the kitchen without knocking, except the door's locked. "Jaysus," he says when he comes up hard against it.

I release the bolt, crack the door: "Sorry Lester, Jaysus isn't here."

But Jane is. Jane, my ghost. The thought makes me grin; the thought of what Lester would say if I told him about her, his Lesterish reaction to even a hint of her. It would be a stream of *Jaysus Marjories* then, followed by: *You ought to have your Christly head examined.* Earlier, I thought I saw Jane, a Jane-shaped glimmer in the curved glass of the china closet. But it might have been a stir of dust from a cat on the fly. They spook easy come evening.

"You might as well come in." I push aside a cat or two, snug the door against their escape and the damp. His cop hat brushes a swag of herbs hung from a kitchen beam, releasing the scent of lemon and a dust of leaves that settles on his shoulders. He twitches. Spider on his neck? Or maybe it's Jane's ghostly finger drawing a cold S along his spine. He brushes herb dust from his sleeve. "Jaysus, Marjorie. What's all this shit?"

"Lemon balm. Thyme. Ladies Mantle. Catnip."

He crosses to the sink, trailing broken leaves. Draws a glass of water, gulps it, sets the glass upside-down in the drainer. Pushes his tongue along the inside of his lower lip, then up into his cheek, like rolling a grape. "There's been some trouble up at the cemetery." He squints through the window at his colleagues, who've surrounded my mailbox and seem to be interrogating it. Raises his hand to signal *all's well.* The woman—Lieutenant Joyce—waves back.

"Why do you think I bolted the door?"

"Thought probably you saw me coming."

"That too." Then, "Uncle Maurice heard it on the scanner. He called, said you closed off the road and I better lock the doors and hide, because you people were working yourselves into a frenzy and somebody might get hurt."

"Friggin' old busybody." Lester picks up the shotgun leaned against the woodbox, checks the load, flips the safety on and off and on. "Did Maurice also inform you that these guys took some serious pot shots at each other? Did he tell you they blew the friggin' angel right off the top of Flutter's monument?"

"Oh no," I say. "Not the friggin' angel."

He lays the gun across the quilted place mat on the table. "Drugs probably. Stealing 'em, selling 'em, inhaling 'em, interjecting 'em. Two of the culprits took off in a van with New York plates. The other one run in the woods. Jaysus Marjorie." His jaw clicks when he sets it hard; the color runs high in his cheeks. "You think this is a joke? There was blood on the grass. Quite a lot of it. These boys mean business."

Behind him, in the arched doorway to the dining room, I've detected a shimmer, like heat rising. Jane taking shape. If Lester turns, he'll see her. If he turns and reaches for her, his hand will pass right through. *Frig this!* he'll say. *Sweet Jaysus.*

But he doesn't turn. He glares at me the way I imagine he glares at suspects, glares them to knee jelly and confession. But I have nothing to confess.

Meanwhile, Jane raises her filmy arm and hand, spreads filmy fingers. She mimes rabbit ears behind the cop hat snug on Lester's big head.

One theory is that Jane moved in when Lester moved out, or soon after.

This spring, to fill Lester-free hours, I cut brush and dug sods between the well and stone wall, unearthing a black marble block, polished on one side, rough on the other. It was four feet long, two feet wide, eight inches thick—like a step or a foundation or even, I thought later, an unfinished gravestone. No engraved words or dates though, just the furrows of the stonecutter's chisel along the edges. Too heavy for me to move alone, I levered it upright, tamped in soil and rocks, and the stone became the centerpiece of my new herb garden.

A few days later, Jane appeared. I was down cellar pulling laundry from the washer, hands draped with wet socks, when I heard something—some soft, definite sound that might have been a cat jumping from a counter, but wasn't. Something like slippers hushing over carpet or a body pushing through a drape. Maybe it was

Lester, sneaking back to reclaim something precious he left behind, like his Roy Orbison albums or his gum- ball machine or his mother's cast-iron fry pan. Probably Lester, reluctant to face the woman who showed him the door.

It wasn't what you think. Not lies. Not stinginess. Not fits of temper or beatings. Not poor hygiene. Not fooling around. Or laziness. Not even sexual dysfunction. Just this: He didn't love me.

Both of us deep into middle-age when we married. Should have known better.

I didn't love him either. Not really. Cold-blooded, melon-headed, hard-bellied chief of friggin' police. I think I was seduced by the aphrodisiac of his police chief power. Either that or I just lost my mind.

A cat followed me up the cellar stairs. We moved quietly, primed for ambush. If it turned out to be Lester, we'd spring out. The cat would hiss and leg it. "Excuse me," I'd say. "I was under the impression you didn't live here any more, Lester."

Lester, startled: a stack of Roy Orbisons avalanching to the floor. His face as red as a Baldwin. *Jaysus Marjorie, give a man a friggin' coronary, why don't ya?*

But it wasn't Lester.

The door at the top of the cellar stairs stood open. The cat and I slipped through it into the hall. I peeked out the porthole window by the weather-sealed front door. No cruiser in the driveway. No Lester.

Down the hall a grid of sunshine from the south-facing window lit the floor, dust motes floating in the stream. Beyond, where the mahogany lowboy darkened the corner, a woman stood—a stranger, strangely familiar. The cat twined my ankle. Another, in a basket, opened her eyes and raised her head, whiskers a-twitch. The woman—in overalls, hair white and floaty—moved toward us. Her movements were floaty, too, as though she were underwater, pushing against a slow strong current. Her face was a blur. I adjusted my glasses, but it didn't help. Her eyes looked as black as my black cat,

Midnight, and tip-tilted. If she cried, her tears would steam past her ears and along the uneven line of her jaw like water from two pitchers.

She stopped at the place where the sunshine touched the floor, stopped short as though she'd reached the edge of a crevasse. A strand of hair, drawn into the sun, lit up like a Fourth of July sparkler and burned away. She smiled, a slight curving of her lips, or the place on her face where her lips must have been. Then she turned, walked into the wall, and merged—quite easily and naturally—with the sprays of wallpaper hyacinths.

"It seems," I said to the cats, "we have ourselves a ghost."

Later, I reasoned that in disturbing the chunk of black marble, maybe I'd disturbed Jane's spirit. Woke her up. Pissed her off. But it also seemed reasonable that her appearance so soon after the unearthing was coincidence, that the stone was just a discarded quarry stone and the blow from my dung fork disturbed nothing but earth and roots. Maybe Jane had been in this house, in this place, all along. Maybe she belonged to this house or the previous one, the eighteenth century cape that burned. Maybe she didn't care to show herself—or maybe I was simply unable to see her—until we rid ourselves of Lester.

Did I tell you my great-great-grandparents built this house on the foundation of the original? In the 1890s. Did I tell you my Great Aunt Molly, childless, left it to me, lock stock and dry-rot, along with enough AT&T stock to pay taxes and then some for the rest of my life? Did I mention Lester wanted to sell this house, invest in a pre-fab log cabin closer to town, sock away the profits for retirement and/or an RV and/or a cross-country trek to Alaska where Lester has always longed to go and catch wild salmon, hunt caribou, eat blubber? Did I mention my reaction to these suggestions?

"Over my rotting corpse," I said.

"Jaysus Marjorie," he said.


Reading in the rocker next to the wood stove by the light of the gooseneck lamp, it occurs to me that with the kitchen lit and the dark outside, people can see in but I can't see out. Lester and his posse maybe, armed to the teeth, outside checking the barn, the woodshed, the outhouse, pressing their noses to my windows. Or the wounded fugitive scouting for a hideout, checking the barn, the woodshed, the outhouse, pressing his nose to my windows. Awful dark out there, a moonless and starless night. Dark in here too, except where the light pools around me. I shiver head to toe: someone walking on my grave.

Sometimes I spook as easily as the cats. It's the curse of imagination.

"Long gone from here," I told Lester. "That guy's hitchhiked to Hill County by now. Halfway to Canada."

"Where could he go? Who's gonna pick him up all blood?" Lester said. "Blood on the grass and a lot of it! He can't get far. Maybe as far as the woods between here and the cemetery, maybe as far as your barn or your friggin' back porch."

"Not my friggin' back porch," I said.

"By rights I should order you out of here for your own safety," he said. "I've got a good mind to evacuate the premises until we get the situation under control."

"Just try it, Lester," I said. "Evacuate me if you can."

"Jaysus Marjorie. Why don't you use your head for once and go spend the night with your Uncle Maurice?"

"The cats and I aren't worried."

"You and your goddamned cats."

Maybe I should turn out all the lights, sit in the dark.

Maybe I should open the window a crack, sit in the dark, listen for a rustle of leaves, the snap of a twig, a moan in the night?

Maybe I should do the friggin' dishes.

I pull on the overhead light, draw hot water into the pan. A cat jumps on the butcher-block. "I fed you already." I nudge the fat boy away. He sails to the floor. The soapy water calms my hands. I wash and rinse the glasses, wash and rinse my plate and the silverware, scrub the burned-on rice from the saucepan. The clock ticks. The refrigerator cycles. I study my reflection in the window over the sink, eyes dark and blurry as Jane's, wire-rimmed glasses, sickle-shaped scar that curves from the corner of my eye to the corner of my mouth.

I let the water drain, scrub the sink with powder. When I was four, the white shepherd in the parking lot of Lucien's Grocery turned on me, his teeth in my face, his breath hot. He had me down before I could make a peep. The doctor said if the bite had been an inch higher, the eye would have been lost. He said if the dog really meant it, he could have torn off my face or gone for my throat.

Growing up, I thought the scar made me so ugly that no man would ever love me. I vowed that if one ever did, I'd never sass him, we'd never argue or fight. And that's how it would be all our lives.

Told you I was cursed with imagination.

I drape the dishcloth over the faucet and open the window a crack. "It *is* stuffy in here," I tell the orange cat named Rabies. "Smells like Lester." Like after-shave and boot polish. Like Lester-sweat and wood smoke.

The crack lets outside in. Damp. Night sounds. I hear something—some soft, definite sound that's not a mole moving under wet leaves, not the sigh of a breeze, not the groan of a tree. Rabies hears it, too. She stiffens. Her tail fluffs. I back away from the window. The cat leaps from the counter to the tabletop, slides into the quilted place mat which slides the shotgun to the edge. "Scaredy cat," I whisper and fold her into my chest. When she struggles to free herself, I set her down and she's gone.

My weight on a weak floorboard sets the chair rocking. I pull the chain of the overhead light. *Lights out. That's better.* I rescue the shotgun from the edge of the table, then switch off the gooseneck lamp. *Now it is as dark inside as out.* The gun stock is warm to my touch, the barrel cold. I settle into the rocker, gun across my lap. I flip the safety switch off and on and off. My index finger strokes the trigger. Night sounds come. A puff of wind in the trees, scratch of forsythia against the clapboards, the murmur of ghostly voices. Too far away, they talk and talk in the walls of this old house, but you can never understand a word they say. Jane, my ghost, on the other hand, gets right up close, but she never says a word.

A car on the road. Crack of tires on gravel. The windows light one after another, blue then dark then blue. Parlor . . . dining room . . . kitchen . . . then dark again. Siren far away, the old Raleigh place, I guess, or somewhere near. Miles by road, closer as the crow flies but rough going through thick woods crisscrossed by stone walls and wetlands.

Phone rings at my elbow.

It's Maurice. "How you making out down there, Belle?" He has called me Belle since I was a baby. In French it means beautiful.

"I'm sitting here in the dark with a shotgun on my lap."

"Just so you stay out of range," he says.

"A cruiser just went by with the lights going."

"They're out in full force. Damn fools. It'll be a wonder if somebody don't shoot themselves or get themselves shot before morning."

"The cats and I are nervous, Maurice. We're not used to all this excitement."

"Friggin' vigilantes," he says.

I dream of cats. I am Molly, Marjorie, Jane in the cellar. The cellar walls, stone embedded in concrete, crumble at a touch. Only stone arches remain, opening to rubble and the herb garden, blooming. Cats everywhere. Strange skeletal cats with waxy flesh and bulging eyes. The woman finds the cat food but can't open the can, not with her fingernails, a knife, pliers. She swings the sledge but the can slides out from under. She gropes, but can't find it and the cats are dying.

I wake in the chair, the shotgun heavy across my knees. Jane stands beside me, her ghostly hand light and cool on my shoulder. She smiles at me. I smile at her. The cats are fine. My chair faces the sealed front door. I can see through the door, which is lucky, because a silhouette is trying to break in, forcing the knob. Apparently in the dark he can't read the sign, "Please use other door." He gnaws at the lock with a screwdriver.

*I've got a gun*, I say. He pauses mid-gnaw, steps back. But instead of retreating, he charges. The door is only paper and he's through, and I stand up so fast the shotgun slides from my lap, and now I *am* awake because the gun hit the floor hard, hair triggered, and the blast shattered Aunt Molly's cookie jar and the kitchen window.

A few minutes later, when Lester pounds the door, I'm tweezing cookie jar from the wall board, thinking maybe I can glue it back together if I find all the pieces.

"Jaysus Marjorie," (pound pound), "what the hell is going on? Who's shot? Jaysus Marjorie, are you in there? You all right? Open the door." (pound pound) "Open the friggin' door."

"Just one friggin' minute."

I open the friggin' door.

There he stands, breathing hard, his hand on the holster strapped to his hip.

"The shotgun went off by accident," I say.

"Jaysus Marjorie." He punches my shoulder, lightly.

"Ow," I say. But it didn't hurt. "I don't know what I ever saw in you, Lester. I don't know why I ever married you. Anybody'd think I was old enough to know better."

"I don't know why you're trying to divorce me," he says.

"You don't love me," I say.

"What the hell ever gave you that idea?" he says. "Jaysus Marjorie."

The phone rings. It's Maurice. "Hey Belle. Just come over the scanner. They apprehended the fugitive over the Old Raleigh place. It's safe to let the cats out."

"Lester's here."

"Friggin' opportunist."

Lester has wandered off. I find him in the parlor, thumbing through the record albums like he owns them, which he does, some of them. "Jaysus Marjorie, you did a job on that kitchen window.

Did you manage to take out a couple of cats in the process, I hope? I could use a cup of coffee," he says. "Long friggin' night."

"You know where the coffee lives."

He slides a 33 from its sleeve, raises the lid on the stereo.

Jane flitters at the foot of the stairs, her filmy hand curling over the newel post, fingers dripping like the whites of raw eggs. Her hair streams, strands of kelp in an invisible current.

"Lester, would you do me a favor?"

"Depends." He's fiddling with the knobs, dropping the record onto the turntable, blowing dust from the needle.

"Would you turn around quick, look over at the stairs and tell me what you see?"

Jane's mouth forms an amazed O. Strands of hair drift across her eyes, her chin, her neck.

Lester places the needle on the record and turns.

Jane raises her filmy arms over her head to make another O. She twirls, a gauzy ballerina, a sparkling funnel.

"I see the stairs," Lester says. "I see a homely painting of your homely Aunt Molly."

Jane swirls and sways, then folds herself into a deep curtsey.

"What else? Look close, Lester. Put on your glasses."

He puts on his glasses.

"I see a plant stand with a half-dead fern hanging down and an ugly orange cat named Rabies thinks she's hid in the leaves, thinks she's going to hook me if I walk by close. I see you Rabies!"

He adjusts the volume on the stereo.

Jane shakes her head, shrugs. The music wells. We all listen, as though for the first time, to the sweet, pure voice of Roy Orbison. A homely fellow, Roy, but such a voice, true as a pewter bell. "In dreams I walk with you-oo," Roy warbles. "In dreams I talk with you-oo."

Jane raises her hand, points her pale index finger into the O of her mouth and pretends to gag.

Lester stares at me, his eyes watery. Roy Orbison always makes him cry. Roy hits the high notes and holds them long and quavery: "But just be-fore the da-awn, I a-wake and find you gone. I can't help it! I can't help it! If I cry-eye-eye . . . "

"Jaysus Marjorie," Lester says in the key of E.

An idea strikes me then, hard as those shotgun pellets struck Aunt Molly's majolica. I guess it strikes Jane, too, because there she flies up to the ceiling like a helium balloon. There she goes through the ceiling and second floor and attic and roof and out into the night, banished, because it has stuck us both that in Lester-talk, *Jaysus Marjorie* means *I love you*. ⅍

# Gram Edie's Tree

THEY'VE TAKEN OFF for the hospital. All still there, far's I know. Come and gone. Been and gone. But has anybody bothered to pick up the phone and let us know what's going on with Uncle Lorus's heart attack—not his first, but maybe his last?

No.

We don't know if he's alive or dead.

So here we sit—Gram Edie and me—wondering. I'm wondering anyway. Who knows what goes on in her head? In four hours, I've managed to spoon about three thimbles-full of chicken noodle soup into her, the noodles curdling over the rim and down her chin. She sips lukewarm tea, looks up at me like she's forgotten who I am. Which she has. "It's me," I say. "Sonya, your favorite granddaughter."

"Oh," she says, "Sonya, what's that thing on your head?"

I touch my head. Almost forgot. Sometimes I do—for a minute or two, even an hour. "It's a silk-screened scarf. I made it myself." I twirl to give her the full effect.

"Where's your hair?"

"It fell out."

"No! Run down to the Bargi-Mart and buy yourself a wig. Here . . ." She reaches into her pocket and pulls out some bills. "You take it."

"Put your money away," I say.

"Well," she says, "if that's the way you're going to be."

I turn on the TV. It's *Swamp Thing*, starring Adrienne Barbeau, who really ought to do something with her hair, sticking out like sprouts. Run a comb through it for goodness sake! I say so to Gram Edie, whose eyes have inexplicably glazed with unshed tears. She sniffs and the tears are reabsorbed. "It would be better," she declares, "if they didn't keep falling down!"

Takes me a minute to realize she's talking about Lorus, whose attack laid him right out on the kitchen floor. "It sure would," I say. "You've got the right idea there, Gram."

Lucky thing Lorus managed to crawl to the telephone, dial next door. Lucky thing Clifford was home. Lucky Clifford's such a big guy. Alice said he had to practically carry Lorus to the car, and Lorus is no lightweight. "Why didn't somebody call an ambulance?" I said. The EMTs could have given him oxygen or injections. They could have jump-started him with paddles if need be. "Didn't anybody think to call an ambulance, Ma?"

"Apparently not," Alice said.

"Lorus didn't want to make a fuss," Cosy said. "You know how he is."

I do. It's how we all are in this family—how we're supposed to be anyway, how we try to be. Our motto: If you have to die (or get married, have a baby, vote Democratic, get divorced, become a lesbian, euthanize your dog, quit your job, move to Maine, come down with cancer), go ahead, just don't make a big fuss about it.

Gram Edie dozes. I half-listen to TV and draw a picture in my book of the lacy curtain in the tall window that looks out on the front yard, the old bench swing hung between twin pines, and the huge mother-pine beyond. The lace curls like a wave. Sideways, my drawing looks like ocean, so I sketch a gull floating on top. I fill in the *TV Guide* crossword, water the fern and pinch off the deads, water the hulking orange tree in the corner. If the bad guys don't get Adrienne Barbeau, the alligators will. There's a huge one rolling like a toothy log just offshore, but of course Adrienne Barbeau's looking the other way. In movies, they're always looking the other way. In life most people can't afford to. I say so out loud even though I'm pretty sure Gram Edie is too dozey to understand.

I draw a picture of the knots on the sooty pine wall behind the wood stove. Funny thing about those knots, they're painted on. It's plain old pine boards that Gram Edie painted to look knotty years ago. Same with the window over the kitchen table. Just paint on plaster, but so real you'd swear you could open that window; you'd swear wild canaries fly in and out of the ever-blooming crabapple tree. If Lorus dies who will take care of Gram Edie? That's the question nobody's asking out loud, but everybody's asking in their heads. And the answer: "Not me." And, "I would but . . ."

We all have good "buts." Mine especially. "I would but I don't know how long I'm going to be around myself."

Well, it's true!

The big mean guy in the movie drank the potion and now he's a small mean piggy guy, because the *Swamp Thing* potion makes you more of what you already are. I hope Adrienne Barbeau doesn't drink it. If she does her teeth will blind with their white, and her breasts will swell as big as Mounts Liberty and Lafayette. I say so to Gram Edie, but she's asleep, head tipped back, mouth open, breath sliding in and out like waves on sand. I sketch her knotty old hand where it has washed up on the arm of the chair.

During commercials, I scrub the kitchen sink, tidy flatware and bag twisties in the drawer. Fix myself a cup of coffee. Adrienne Barbeau lets out a screech; Gram Edie startles awake, surprised to see me on the couch with my coffee. She's looking around for Lorus.

"It's Sonya," I say. "Remember me?"

"What's that thing on your head?"

She touches her own hair to make sure it's still there. Gram Edie is a touch vain about her hair, always has been. She's colored it for at least forty years. It's a kind of purpley-auburn at the moment, and combed forward on her face like a wig on an applehead doll. She hasn't been able to color it herself for some time, so cousin Cosy, the cosmetologist, makes house calls.

"What a card!" Cosy says of Gram Edie. "If I don't do everything just right, just the exact same way I did it the time before, she's on my case, honest to God. 'What's in that bottle? What's that noise? What's that clippy thing? Get that off my head. What are you *doing* to me?'

" 'What do you think I'm doing?' I say. 'Making you gorgeous, of course.'

" 'Oh,' she says. 'That's all right, then. Proceed.' "

Gram Edie has risen from her chair. She slip-slides beside me on the couch, pokes a finger up under my scarf. "No hair," she says.

"Really?" I say. "Where do you suppose it got to?"

"Where's my son Lorus?"

"Lorus got sick. They've taken him to the hospital."

"Who has?"

"Clifford drove him. Clifford from next door. And after that Alice came by—your daughter Alice, my mother, you remember Alice—and Walter and Cosy and Cosy's little baby, Peaches. It was Grand Central Station around here. Everybody wanted to check how you were doing. Peaches drooled on you and spit up on poor Walter because he has no idea how to hold a baby. Little devil snagged my glasses and threw them on the floor; it's a wonder they didn't break. Then they all went to the hospital to check on Lorus, except me. They left me here to keep an eye on you."

She squeezes my wrist. "Where's Lorus?"

"How about some chicken noodle soup?"

She makes a face like it's goat pee.

Before they left for the hospital I asked if there were any special instructions. "Just don't let her near the stove," Alice said. "Sometimes the pilot doesn't work, and she tries to cook but forgets to light the burner. One day Lorus came home—he'd just run down to the store for half a minute—and the house reeked of gas. She was asleep in her chair. He thought she'd succumbed."

"It's a wonder he didn't drop dead on the spot," Cosy said. "The shock of seeing her laid out like that and thinking she'd succumbed."

"Keep her away from the woodpile," Walter said. "She gets it in her head sometimes to chop kindling and out to the woodshed she goes. Almost chopped her thumb off last spring."

"It was dangling by a thread," Cosy said. "She came in the house looking for a band-aid."

"Lorus hid the hatchet," Alice said.

"If I know her," Walter said, "she'll find it. If she decides she wants it, she'll find it."

"What a card!" Cosy said.

"Try to get her to eat something if you can," Alice said. "She doesn't eat much. You eat like a bird, don't you, Mother? I said to Lorus, try some of those nutrition milk shakes for old people like they advertise on television. I don't know what he was thinking, letting her go so far down hill. My goodness," squeezing Gram Edie's loose-knuckled hand, "you're skin and bone, Mother, nothing but skin and bone."

Gram Edie snatched back her hand and tucked it in her pocket. Peaches started to cry, a whimper that amplified to a wail.

"Who's pinching that child?" Gram Edie said. "Walter, are you pinching that baby?"

"She's hungry." Cosy fingered the buttons on her blouse. "I'll feed her in the car. O.K., Peaches? Are you hungry, sweet thing?"

YES, Peaches wailed. I AM VERY HUNGRY. FEED ME NOW.

"Such stories they tell," Gram Edie says. "What possesses these people to tell such stories? Especially Lorus. I think p'rhaps we made too much of him when he was small. He's the baby, you know."

"He's your sixty-five-year-old bouncing baby Bub," I say. "Or is it sixty-six?"

She recounts the story I've heard a hundred times about how Lorus won first prize in the Beautiful Baby Contest at the Grange Fair when he was nine months old. He was a stunning baby, she says: eyes wide apart and alert; ears smooth and flat, like cucumber slices on the sides of his head, that's how perfect those little ears were. "He was awful cunning," she says.

"Still is," I say.

After he won the blue ribbon, the other children called him Bouncing Blue-Ribbon Baby Bub. They were merciless, but after a while the nickname shortened to just Bub, which some in the family still call him today. "What kind of a name is that for a person," Gram Edie says. "Bub!"

"Easy to spell," I say. "Even if you spell it backwards. Even if you spell it upside down. Even if you spell it standing on your head."

Gram Edie is alarmed: "We'll have none of that in this house."

She looks at the TV, the wood stove, the piano nobody plays anymore though the keys are worn to nubs from so much playing over the years. She looks at the orange tree hulking in the corner. "Where's Lorus? Where's my son?"

I locate a bottle of sherry under the sink. Pour each of us a nip. Now we sip and wait for the call. Surely some one of them will call soon to let us know if he's alive or dead. You'd think one of them would. Common courtesy dictates.

"Years ago," Gram Edie says, "you were just a little girl sitting cross-legged on that rug; just a little bit of a thing eating an orange. Peel scattered every which way, juice dribbling down your front. You were having a grand time until you swallowed a seed. Lorus said a tree was going to grow in your tummy. You didn't like that idea one bit, so your father went out in the garden and came back with a bucket of dirt. He extracted another seed, planted it, set the bucket in the corner, and there it sits still. Who knew that seed would take? Look at the size of that monstrosity."

"That was my mother, Gram. It was Alice who swallowed the orange seed."

The sherry is sweet. It warms my bones. Gram Edie seems to be enjoying hers, too. She drinks it down, then holds out her glass for another. "Dare I?" she says.

We dare.

Gram Edie and I have moved ourselves outside into the soft air of almost dusk. We sit together on the bench swing, the needles of the twin pines raining pine fragrance over us. I've left the front door open so we'll hear the telephone if it rings. Not that anybody'd bother to pick up the phone and let us know what's going on; ease our minds, one way or the other. Damned inconsiderate, I say. Damned strange, too. It's almost as if when they went they really *went*. Not just to County Hospital ten miles down the road, but to another place altogether. It's as if Gram Edie and I are the only ones left in this small world of bench swing, twin pines, needle carpet, the big old mother-pine across the yard. It's as if the rest—everything but us—is painted on plaster. The house. The road. The swamp across the way. I can hear the peepers though, so the swamp must be real.

No cars on the road, though. No neighbors at Clifford's or the new log cabin. No County Hospital. No Alice, Walter, Cosy, Peaches. No Lorus. No Adrienne Barbeau. No Swamp Thing. Nor even the memory of them. Just the peepers and Gram Edie and me.

"Have you been taking your medicine?" she says.

"Oh yuh. And a lot of it, too."

"You take your medicine," she says. "You keep on taking it. It'll do you good."

"Are you warm enough, Gram?" She's seems to be curling in on herself. Shrinking.

She thinks for a moment. Plucks at the sleeve of her sweater. Notices her hand. Studies it. "Isn't that awful?" she says. "Skin and bones." She rolls back the sleeve of her sweater, holds out her arm. Looks it over. Raises her legs so she can see her ankles and the loose felt slippers.

"Where's the rest of me?" she says. "You can see my veins. You can see my bones. Am I a ghost yet?"

"Am I?"

We swing. Her hands fold in her lap, legs dangling. She dozes. Maybe I doze, too. Must have, because when I open my eyes it's dark and Gram Edie's face hovers no more than two inches from mine. She's trying to figure out who or what I am and what the heck I'm doing here. "Oh," she says, "it's you. I was worried. Thought you'd succumbed."

"Not yet," I say.

"I'm almost ninety years old," she says. "Can you believe it?"

I correct her. "Ninety-seven."

"You don't get to be this old by looking the other way, Sonya."

I'm delighted she remembers. "That's right. I'm Sonya."

"Of course, you are," she says. "Who else would you be?"

"Sonya," she says and kisses the back of my hand. This is a surprise. A shock even. But sweet. Ours is not a kissy family, nor a huggy one; since nobody's looking I give her a little squeeze across the shoulders. We sit shoulder to shoulder. She's looking away now, squinting at that big old mother-pine across the yard as if it just appeared, as if she's never laid eyes on it before, as if she's never seen anything like it. She leans forward so hard I have to plant my toes to keep the swing from spilling us out plunk on the ground.

"See how they go together," she says of the tree. She extends her arms, twines them loosely, fingers spread and curving away one hand from the other. "See," she says.

I look at the shape her arms describe. That big old mother-pine, I realize, is really two grown together, and each has become—over the course of a century or two—more of what it already was. And something entirely different, too. Big old twisted tree, two trunks grown together, dancers embracing. From them, tens of limbs and hundreds of branches reach up and out, like Gram Edie's fingers reaching up and out, curving away one from another like Gram Edie's hands.

"Where's Lorus?" she says. "Oh, he's in the house. I can see him in the window. Hello, Lorus." She waves. "Is that you, Lorus?" she calls. "That's Lorus," she says. "That's my son, Lorus."

I don't see him. Wish I could.

Somewhere, far away, a telephone is ringing. It's saying, COME IN THE HOUSE RIGHT NOW, SONYA; PICK UP THIS PHONE, AND HEAR THE BAD NEWS.

It rings and rings.

Gram Edie doesn't hear it.

And after a while neither do I. ❧

## The Characters in Dreams End and Their Family Connections

Elizabeth Moynihan Hamilton (*Grammie Old's mother*) *m.* ? Hamilton

*Her sisters:*
Rosa May Moynihan
Molly Sarah Moynihan

Eff P. Hamilton (*brother to Grammie Old*)

Grammie Old *aka* Julia Moynihan Hamilton Forbes *m.* Martin C. Forbes

Lucretia G. Forbes

Smith M. Forbes

Si M. Forbes *m.* Clarabelle

Hamilton D. Forbes *m.* Priscilla K. Olmstead

Miriam R. Forbes *aka* Mim

Boy

Hamilton Jr. *aka* Ham *m.* Sara Lovering

Prudence *aka* Poppy *m.* Jim (and others)

Barbara Forbes

Lucy Rose *m.* tall man

Red-headed baby

# Dreams End

*193–*

### BOY

LOVES HIS MOTHER and father, the homestead called Dreams End, and his room in the attic where the ceiling almost meets the floor and one tall, thin-paned window overlooks the meadow. He loves the peach tree at the window when the leaves unfurl, when the blossoms pop, when fruit sags the branches, when bare branches scratch the glass like whisperings. He loves the field, the orchard, the river, the waxy lilies with yellow hearts floating on Small Pond. He loves Chip-dog who pees for joy at the sight of him, twines his legs and jumps up delicately like dancing. He loves his aunts, uncles, cousins and the smiley lady who checks them through at the grocery, her hair stiff as tinsel, eyelids powdery, a pin on her chest that spells her name. She asks after the rest of the family, because she was once married to a distant relation who died young of blood poison. Boy can't remember who told him so—one of the cousins probably, Mim or Poppy or Ham—but he wishes they hadn't, because now when he sees the smiley lady he thinks *blood poison,* and a bad feeling settles thick as the dust Aunt Lucretia found when she lifted the top off the upright to look for something lost.

Mim, small then, said: "Mother, there's moss growing in the piano," tiptoe on the bench, peering into the wire and wood guts.

"How did it get *so* dusty?" Lucretia said.

Mim traced her name on the backboard. Boy traced a B as big as his hand. B for Boy. The dust held together like felt on the hammers, thick, like the bad feelings about blood turned to poison, poison all through you, part of you. He wonders if poison blood is red like regular blood. Or golden. Or purple with blue dots like the salamander under the woodpile. Trouble is when your blood turns to poison there's no way to get rid of it. His mother opened all the windows and doors to get rid of the bats, to show them where outside was. Dreams End filled with mosquitoes. The whole house buzzed, and no one slept. That wouldn't work for blood though—opening your veins like windows—because your life is in your blood and when your blood is gone so are you.

He tries not to imagine being blood poisoned, being gone. Thinks instead of the peach tree, the river, Chip-dog. But he can't forget about the bad thing that happened to the smiley lady's husband, hurrying after a beeline, barbed wire stretched stone to stone bit through his pants and shin. The wound didn't bleed. The leg turned blue and red and yellow.

"Yellow's the worst," Boy's father says. "It's poison built up inside. Should have lanced it right then."

"Then it would have gotten worse infected," Boy's mother says.

"How could it have been any worse? He died, Clarabelle. Poor bastard friggin' died."

Boy's mother makes a bad-language face.

"All they had to do was fill a washtub with hot water and Epsom salt," Boy's father says. "Stick his leg in, sit there and soak, and don't move, so the poison don't get to your heart while it still has kick. That's what Mother did when any of us kids hurt ourselves. Epsom salt and stay the hell put. Worked for us, didn't it? We're still kicking, ain't we? Except for Hamilton. But Epsom salt can't do much for what ailed him. Nothing much you can do for a man struck by lightning."

Boy can't remember much about his Uncle Hamilton—Ham and Poppy's father—struck dead on Small Pond when Boy was little, Ham and Poppy babies. Just that he was big, with a beard dark as his eyes, and a voice that rumbled so you could hardly understand a word he said.

One pearly cloud in a clear sky, and Hamilton fishing in the middle of Small Pond during the Mayfly hatch. Others, too, fishing from shore and boats. One bolt of white-hot lightning snapped out of that pearly cloud, struck Hamilton Forbes Senior dead on the spot and sent fireballs skittering over water gray as slate. No warning. No thunder. No rain before or after. Didn't even set the boat on fire, though the middle seat scorched.

The trout paid no attention. Kept right on biting, crazy for May-flies. But the fishermen reeled in.

"You can't cure blood poison with Epsom salt, Si," Boy's mother says. "It's in the blood. They have to treat the blood."

The smiley lady's husband, poor soul (Boy's mother calls him), ended up in County Hospital where the poor bastard (Boy's father calls him) suffered the tortures of hell until he died. A man scrapes his shin on barbed wire, gets carted off to County Hospital, and a week later he's dead. "They take you to that hell hole," Boy's father says, "you don't come home. They take you there to die, that's why. Better off home than butchered."

"You're scaring him, Si," Boy's mother says.

"You *be* scared, Boy. You be good and scared. Steer clear of that place. They come after you—you run."

Boy smells blood. It is the smell that stays on the ground long after the fresh-shot deer is dragged away. Butchers, Boy thinks. Hell hole. Like a shiner trap. The shiners swim unsuspecting in and they can't swim out.

"Boy," his mother is saying. "Come back."

He hasn't really gone away. Hasn't moved an inch. Right there in the same place, same position, cross-legged on the edge of the braided rug. His mother and father hover over him, their two big faces close together and alike. Boy says, "I went away, but now I'm back."

Time has passed. The clock on the wall clicked off minutes; he doesn't know how many. He went *somewhere*, but only in his mind. Grammie Old calls it dreaming awake. She says it happens to her, too. No one seems to mind that it happens to her, maybe because she's old, but when Boy goes away, his mother worries sick, and his father swears a blue streak. "Jesus," his father says. "Jesus H. Christ."

"Not his fault, Si." Boy's mother touches the knob of his elbow. Boy touches back to make sure she's real, he's real.

"Sweet Jesus," his father says. "Sweet suffering Christ."

*Dreams End Estate Auction, August 24, 1991*

MIM

Wants that cigar box of buttons for the rag-haired dolls she sews from scraps—her latest, Evangeline, sitting in her lap right now getting her pantaloons hemmed. Tiny needle; tiny stitches. Mim will use the buttons to fasten doll vests and skirts or just for decoration. The silks and velvets, too, nests of fabric in the drawers of the spindle-legged sewing cabinet.

She wants them. She deserves them. She will have them.

George, the auctioneer, holds up an apple-shaped pin cushion with felt stem and leaves. He rattles the button tin, marvels at the needle-scarred beeswax, brown and hard as amber almost. Mim jumps in at twenty-five dollars. Too much? Not for Grammie Old's pin cushion. Not for the awl. Not for the darning egg Boy named "Buddy," and scratched eyes, nose and mouth in soft pencil on hard wood. Not for the sheaf of embroidery thread with which she will knot features on blank muslin faces.

Cousin Poppy bids thirty.

Mim pokes the fat old bat in the shoulder: "I'm bidding."

Poppy doesn't even turn her head. "So am I."

"Give her hell, Mim," Cousin Ham says.

She ignores him. They all ignore him, except his girlfriend Grenadine (pushing fifty, hardly a girl), who says: "Hush, Ham," and smiles as sugary as her cotton-candy hair. She pretends to be a Southern belle, but Mim knows for a fact she was born in Colebrook, New Hampshire. Her lips and a border of skin around them are slathered cinnamon-red, her upper plate bleached a shocking white. Grenadine is not her real name; it's what the family calls her among themselves. They all feel bad for Sara, not a blood relation but married to Ham so long she seems like one, and swept aside after thirty-eight years of marriage, traded in like an outdated refrigerator.

THIRTY-DOLLAR-BID-A-DOLLAR-WHERE-A-DOLLAR-FORTY-HOWBOUT-THIRTY-FIVE?

Mim raises her bidding card.

NOW THE FORTY . . .

Poppy nods.

"Fifty!" Mim says.

FIFTY-DOLLARS-THE-BID.

A pewter-haired dealer in the row behind whispers into Mim's ear, "You'll be sorry."

He smells like the sea. She falls in love.

"I'm already sorry," she says. "But I can't help myself."

"Maybe you should try harder, dear." He says it this way: *dee-ah*.

She falls out of love.

This is why she's never married.

Poppy bids fifty-five.

"Mumma," says Poppy's girl, Lucy—her redheaded baby swooped in a tummy pack; his bottom round and heavy as fruit. "Did you realize you're bidding against Cousin Mim?"

"I realize it," Poppy says.

Poppy's fourth husband, Jim, says: "Maybe you girls should split the difference. Each pay half—one take the cabinet; one take the contents?"

Ham pokes him in the shoulder: "Hey Jim. That's a good idea!"

AND SIXTY?

"Yes," says Mim.

"Stubborn!" Ham says. "Did you ever see any two so stubborn?"

"It's scary," Jim says.

"Runs in the family," Lucy says.

"Ham's not stubborn," Grenadine says. "He's a big-ole puffcake. You're just a big-ole puffcake, aren't you, honey?"

Poppy turns her head: "My god Mim, are you still bidding? I thought you dropped out. I should think you would."

"I should think *you* would."

ARE YOU TWO LADIES TOGETHER?

"No," they say.

Poppy presses her nose to the back of her grandchild's fuzzy skull.

Lucy says: "Don't breathe on him! Germs, Mumma!"

AND FIVE.

Poppy says to Lucy: "I've had this cold too long to give it." She whispers in the baby's rubbery ear: "Your mother's such a fuming worrywart. I hope she doesn't give you neurotics."

AND SEVENTY.

Mim nods.

Poppy glares. When they were kids Poppy's evil eye scared Mim, a little. Not anymore: "Poppy, put your card away. And don't you dare raise it again."

Poppy dares.


*1951*

## GRAMMIE OLD

Called Martin's wild-eyed hounds home with a yoo-hoo and quieted them with a glance. They say she could do the same with Martin. She predicted storms well before ground wind silvered the leaves, knew the length of a season better than *Old Farmer's Almanac*, sensed a full moon in the tingle of her scalp, whispered secrets in cats' ears: sometimes, the cats whispered back. For inspiration and guidance, she consulted invisibles no one else saw or heard. They say she could even conjure ghosts.

For all her sensitivities, Grammie suffered headaches—even as a child—that laid her flat out on the bed in the middle of the day. Sometimes (she confided) her skull seemed about to explode. A weaker person might have wished it.

"The garden will just have to wait," she said to Mim, then a young woman, visiting the folks at the homestead. Grammie was already old. Some would say she'd been old forever. She'd buried Martin when she was thirty-one, raised their children without him. She would outlive her brother, her eldest son, her daughter, even her grandson Boy. But she didn't let sorrow embitter her, though it troubled her deeply when people died out of order. She refused to let trials hold her back or slow her down, and remained nimble well

into her nineties, tending her side-hill garden, even when the time
came that when she bent to pull weeds, she'd stay bent awhile. The
up-and-down bothered, she said, more than the bending and staying put. Others offered to weed around the strawberries, thin the
carrots, but she shooed them off: "The more I do," she said, "the
more I *can* do." She loved herbs especially, for their fragrance and
tenacity. Thyme rooted between stones. Parsley thriving in soil so
sandy you wouldn't think there was any goodness to it. Mint that
thickened and spread every time you cut it, and kind of a nuisance,
too: mint would take over the whole garden if you let it, maybe
even the world!

The day of Mim's visit, Grammie was in her room, resting in the
pressed-backed rocker painted ivory. Her face was ivory, too, except
for the mauve line of her lips and hollows at cheek and temple. She
looked like a little old ghost wrapped in a bright afghan. The room
was dark except for slits of sunlight at the edges of the drawn shades.
The old woman's eyes were closed. The back of her skull dented a
feather pillow, her forehead drawn and pale as a boiled potato. Mim
sat low on the tapestry footstool, arms wrapped around her knees.
The room felt clammy—too damp for a sick old lady, but Grammie
insisted she was warm enough, perfectly comfortable, she said, except for her head: "Big as the moon, Mim. Probably doesn't look it,
but it is." She wasn't complaining, but seemed full of wonder.

"A reprieve for the weeds," Mim said.

"Some call my herbs nothing *but* weeds." Grammie opened ir-
idescent eyes. "Can you imagine?" Then the lids, heavily veined,
shuddered down. Mim, unnerved, imagined she could see the
veins throbbing. Course she couldn't. Yellow-birch hands nested in
Grammie's lap; Mim wanted to touch them, warm them. Course
she didn't.

Mim said, "Can I bring you a cup of medicine tea?"

"I've had tea," Grammie said. "Tea, tea, and more tea. Clarabelle
spoons it down my gullet by the quart. Another spoonful, I'll float
out the window."

Mim wanted to curve her hand over Grammie's skull and draw

the suffering from that little old head into her own body. Course she didn't. Couldn't. Others in the family had gifts—Grammie, Boy, Uncle Smith—but Mim . . . full of good intentions and that was as far as it went.

"Nothing to *be* done, Mim." Grammie's hands flittered over the afghan, bunching it, smoothing it. "Nothing at all," as though that were a fine thing as well as true.

*August 24, 1991*

### MIM

Climbed out of the wagon, paused to extract her folding chair and basket from the way-back, locked five doors. She heard the river in the distance, a sound so constant, low and smooth, most people didn't. She heard it the minute she set foot in Si's neglected, dew-soaked hayfield. A soft sound and familiar. *Forget the auction, Mim,* the river called. *It's cool and quiet down here. You could swim!* But she'd come all this way to auction and, by God, auction she would.

"Can't do it," she said out loud, since no one was close enough to hear. "Duty calls." She high-stepped field stubble, following the pack toward Dreams End and the auction tent. She moved slowly, almost timidly, down hill, because of the time she toppled and broke her wrist. It was a long, tricky walk across the field to the auction site: uneven terrain, uneven rows of cars, trucks, trailers to maneuver. Si's beautiful hayfield turned into a parking lot.

She'd tried to persuade Sara to come along, called early, ample warning but not so far in advance Sara would have time to stew. In Mim's opinion, the woman needed to get out more. Be among people. Even relatives. "I don't think so," Sara said. "Groceries to buy. Curtains to hem. I've got a lot doing today."

"The auction only lasts one day," Mim said. "This is the *only* day. If you're worried about Ham and Grenadine being there, so what if they are. You have as much right to walk the Earth as they do."

"I'm not going," Sara said.

"Stubborn," Mim said.

"Not stubborn," Sara said. "Busy."

"If I do see them," Mim said, "I might just have to say something. I'm not very happy with Ham at the moment and I never liked Grenadine. I might just have to say something."

"Don't you say anything."

"I might not be able to hold back."

"Well you better had."

Driving to the auction alone, Mim fumed over Sara's stubbornness for five miles, rehearsed for ten the truths she'd inflict on faithless Ham and slutful Grenadine. Then she got over it, pretty much. Life's too short.

Safe at the bottom of the rollingest hill in the hayfield, she spotted a young man with an orange cap and gloves directing a Ford truck into the dip. "Big mistake," Mim said to herself. And it was. The truck sank in the sog. Couldn't that young man tell by the green of the grass how wet that spot would be? What ailed him? The driver glowered and spun his wheels. The young man balled his gloved hands on his hips, shook his head. "Get ready," he called, shoulder to the tailgate. "Give it the gas!"

Wheels turned in place. Mud flew. The young man jumped back, splattered. He wiped a lick of mud from his mouth, revealing a mustache like a crow feather. Mud striped his jeans and Auctions-by-George T-shirt.

"A spring bubbles up right there," Mim informed him.

"There's no bottom to it," the driver said. "More I spin, the deeper she goes." The truck had sunk to its axle. Uncle Si would have a fit if he knew the treatment his beautiful hayfield was getting. He'd had a hot temper in life; no reason to suppose he wouldn't in death as well. She imagined his furious old bones rattling the coffin. And Aunt Clarabelle, in the side-by-side plot, disturbed by the commotion. Poor old woman. Poor old folks, the two of them, would they ever rest in peace?

Course Si hadn't rested much during the last decades of his life either. Clarabelle said he didn't sleep at all for a year after Boy died. Which couldn't be right, could it? She said Si would lie down for a while at ten or eleven each night, but by midnight he'd be wandering upstairs and down, out to the barn, across the hayfield, cross-country to the river or the wood lot, a mile down the logging road to Small Pond. Pitch black, rain or snow, wind or freeze—never took a lantern or a flashlight. Maybe he was sleepwalking. If so, his sense of direction stayed awake, because he always found his way home by dawn.

Clarabelle believed he was searching for Boy. She confided this to Mim. For all she knew, Clarabelle said, Boy's ghost was out and about, too.

"I hope you're going to fill in those ruts," Mim said to the orange-capped man with the crow feather mustache. "I trust you're not going to leave the ground all torn up like that."

"It'll be perfect," he promised. "We'll put it all back perfect and smooth it over and the grass'll grow; you'll never know we were even here; you'll never know the difference."

*Oh,* she thought, disheartened, *but I will.*


*August 24, 1991*

### BARBARA

Finds boxes of linens in disarray. A fallen handkerchief, lace-edged, delicate as web. E.M.H. embroidered white on white. She realizes this scrap of fabric once belonged to Elizabeth Moynihan Hamilton, great-great-grandmother known as Lizzie. Grammie Old's mother. In her hands Barbara holds something older than Grammie, who was so old when Barbara knew her, she seemed like always.

A thread catches in Barbara's thumbnail. Brad thought her hands were ugly. Blunt. He didn't say so, but he painted them that way—stubby hands with cactus fingers. And her face didn't fare much better, the features flat, coarse, hair like toasted straw.

"Not ugly, Barbara," he said. "Intriguing."

"Ugly," she said.

"Maybe how you see the painting is how you see yourself."

"No," she said. "That's not it."

She tugs at the thread but gently—better to tear the nail than the lace. The handkerchief smells of age and lilac talc, like Grammie Old and the dark corner room in which she spent the last years of her life. She always kept a hankie like this one—her mother's han-kie!—tucked in the rolled cuff of her cardigan, one corner fluting out. Barbara balls it in her hand and the fabric is so fine it practically disappears. Poof, and it is tucked in her pocket.

"Excuse me."

*Caught!*

A woman with hair as big and pale as her straw bag elbows Bar-bara aside. It's Grenadine, her father's lover. Not caught, but tipped by Grenadine's bulk and her own recoil into a quilt-draped drying rack. "Have you talked to your daddy?" Grenadine says. "He thinks you're mad at him. You're not mad at him are you? He wants to give you a big old honey-bear hug, just in case." She picks up a chamber pot, white with golden vines wreathing the base. "I'n't that a pretty thing? Delicate. Wouldn't it make a gorgeous fruit bowl all cleaned up, and set pretty on your daddy's hutch? Or a candy dish. Too big for Canada mints; my goodness, it'd hold a year's supply."

"It's a piss pot," Barbara says. "You want to put candy in a piss pot, go right ahead."

"It *i'n't!*" A twitch scrambles Grenadine's face. "It *is?* Well, it's pretty just the same!" She turns away. A barrette, like a small bird, nests in the bulge of her hair. Barbara plucks at the the quilt, releas-ing scents of cedar and mothballs, a hint of apple. The quilt is stiff with age and dust; a collage of matted velvets, shattered silks, feath-er-stitched. The backing is tea-stained homespun, spiral quilted. This quilt is as crazy as Grammie herself had been, or her mother, Elizabeth, known as Lizzie. A quilt as crazy as Barbara sometimes believes she herself could be. Must be crazy, scoffing up Lizzie's handkerchief! Squirreling it away like a sneak-thief, when she could just as well have bid on it. How much could an antique hankie sell for? A dollar? Two? She must be crazy for defacing Brad's mural the way she did. He's an artist for godsake. But it was *her* bedroom wall. She'd walked in, thrown down her suitcase, kicked off her shoes, turned, and there they were: four moonfaced women, mainly na-ked, stretched floor to ceiling. One embraced the door casing, long fingers tangled in weedy hair that curled over her shoulders, down her back, all the way to the knob. Two pirouetted on impossibly long legs with muscled calves and engorged toes. One ran up an invisible hill in a translucent caftan, gazing back over her shoulder with mad-woman eyes and an angel smile. Barbara kind of liked that one, but not enough to spare her. "Jesus," Barbara had said. "Sweet suffering Christ."

She'd pulled her shoes back on, driven to the hardware store, bought a gallon of flat white and a roller. Apparently these gro-tesques lived in her lover's imagination, but by God, she didn't have to look at them, and she was damned sure she didn't want them looking at her. The cactus-finger portrait had been one straw. The women on the wall were the last.

He hadn't taken it well.

She may be crazy—or well on her way—but she's not sorry, not sorry for having given Brad the heave-ho, not sorry she stole (is in the process of stealing) Grammie's mother's handkerchief. She may buy the quilt, too, maybe for her own mother who stayed away to keep the peace—Sara would deny it, but it's true. Maybe for her own mother, Barbara will buy this marvelous something created from a thousand almost-nothings.

"Raggedy old thing," Grenadine observes. "Falling to pieces."

Barbara returns the quilt to the rack. Wistful. It will probably sell for more than she can afford. Now that she's paying the full freight for rent and utilities, she can't afford much. And she needs to save. Needs to save for the changed future.

She moves among crates of musty books, running her fingers over spines. There's the famous pine cradle, its hand-carved rockers worn nearly flat. Legend has it Martin built the cradle as a wedding gift for Grammie, and that all their children (some grandchildren, too) had the use of it. She pictures Smith and Si swaddled side-by-side. It's not that hard to imagine those wizened old men as wrinkley-faced babies squawking through twin infancy. And Great Aunt Lucretia, plump and rosy, so like Mim, they say, that to see Mim at sixty is to see the image of her mother, right down to the constellation of moles on her soft, wide neck. And Barbara's own grandfather, Hamilton, whom she knows only from the story of his untimely death, the unlucky boat stored in the rafters of the barn, hoisted there and hammocked in ropes. She supposes it will be sold, too, and the buyers (unless they're family, and who in the family would want it?) won't realize.

She navigates a maze of trunks on trunks, chests on chests, bureaus, dilapidated bow-back chairs. Floor lamps like street markers. All familiar. All strange. And strangers, dealers, rummaging as though this stuff already belonged to them. Portrait of a family. Dissolving. Dissolved. Uncle Si's taxidermy collection—partridge, pheasant, woodcock; mink and squirrels poking their heads out of drawers; an albino fisher-cat, a red fox. Deer heads, antlered and mounted. A tangle of headless antlers nearby.

When Barbara was little and Mother or one of the aunts insisted on a visit to Grammie's room, the worst part was passing the highboy with Si's critters arranged on and around it. The fox was the worst.

Barbara's hand viced in an adult grip, she tried to walk fast, but the hall was a hundred miles long and the closer they got to the highboy and the open door of Grammie's room, the heavier her feet became. Mother or the aunt would grow impatient. "Come on, Barbara. Stand up now. Walk right along. If you're good, Grammie might give you a chocolate."

A jar of chocolates on the bed stand, when Barbara picked one, she'd hope for something besides vanilla inside—cherry, nougat, caramel. But no. Always the same: a waxy chocolate skin over a dollop of vanilla paste. She accepted the chocolates when offered (it would have been rude not to), but she didn't like them. If she ate one now, it would probably make her sick. The thought turns her stomach. In fact, she may vomit on the fox—musty, infested, molting—staring at her now as it had then. Then she would press herself to the wall trying not to meet its glassy eyes but, most always, unable to resist a glance.

She shudders: someone walking on her grave? No, she thinks, other people's graves. It is as if Si—or some soulful part of him—keeps an eye on the taxidermies. As if Grampa Hamilton fishes still from his boat, waiting for a trout to rise to the bit of feather, thread and glue on his line. Clarabelle is here, too, in the porcelain curve of her favorite teapot. And Aunt Lucretia, Grammie, Martin, Eff who died of drink, Boy who died the year Barbara was born. Grammie always said Barbara had a lot of Boy in her—not reincarnation exactly, but something like. She imagines family spirits tethered to these things, their things. Spirits like balloons that could drift off, but don't. A side-crank Victrola, ornate in three veneers, light curving over dark. Beautiful thing; she can't remember having seen it before. Who did it belong to. Where was it kept? What kind of music did it play? Did anybody dance? She lifts the domed lid. On the turntable, which is not turning but for a moment seems to be, a rat stretches to its ratty length. Not just a rat, but a *big* son-of-a-bitch. Big as a small cat.

Practically mummified, it is the deadest thing she has ever seen. Deader than any of Si's gruesome taxidermies, and so well-preserved that for a moment she thinks it, too, might have come under his knife and been doused in formaldehyde.

She stifles whatever was about to come out of her mouth—a scream, a laugh, both. She swallows her horror like a cracker, chokes it down. Tufts of reddish hair on strips of leatherized skin, splinter of bone where a leg has separated from the torso. "Nice," she says. And lets the lid fall heavily back into place.

"Barbara," her father says in her ear.

"Jesus," she says.

"No, it's just me." He's standing too close. She can smell his aftershave, feel the push of his shoulder into hers. He cocks his head: "How you doing?"

"Fine."

"You find something you want to buy? Anything you can't live without? Stuffed squirrel? Pineapple bedstead? Pair of andirons? How about your Uncle Si's railroad cap? George calls it memorabilia. He says anything railroad's collectible."

"That's sick," she says. "Selling Uncle Si's cap he wore every day of his life." She feels sick. "Who would even want it but him?"

"Si's got no more use for it. And, hey, who can afford to be sentimental? Not me. But, Barbara . . . Barbara, if there's something you want in particular, you go ahead and bid it—I'll deduct it off my percentage." Each of the nephews and nieces—Poppy, Mim and Barbara's dad, Ham—inherited a third. Since they couldn't agree on who would get what among the personal assets, the deal was to put it all on the block, so each of the heirs could bid off what he or she wanted, and split the money at the end. "Don't say no, Barbara. Just pick out something nice. O.K?"

"I don't know," she says.

"Come on," he says. "It would mean a lot to me."

Tears in his eyes? Probably allergies. But if they are tears of regret, it's a little late. A lot late. "If you want to buy something, buy Grenadine that piss pot over there," she says. "She likes it. Go right ahead. If you want to deduct something, deduct the piss pot, Daddy. It'll make her day."

*August 24, 1991*

### POPPY

Says, "Oh-my-god. Over there by Grammie's lilacs. With the cap. He looks about a hundred years old."

"He is," Ham says. "Close to."

It's Uncle Smith. Terrible aged. Either that or Si's ghost has appeared among them. The sight of the old man squinting at nothing, as if he were all alone in the world instead of smack in the middle of an auction, gives Poppy the willies. *Oh-my-sweet-God-in-heaven,* she thinks, *maybe it is Si's ghost.* The same thought occurs to Mim and Evangeline, who hides her face in Mim's lap. Mim strokes her purple hair, strips of knotted wool sewn in rows to Evangeline's muslin scalp. Poppy shakes herself. Course it's not a ghost. Just Smith being standoffish. He toddled up the road to see the goings-on but, as usual, wants nothing to do with the rest of them. "Uncle Si would be rolling in his grave," Poppy says, "if he knew his brother was on the premises."

"Where'd you say the old coot was?" Jim asks.

"Over by the lilacs," Poppy says. "Do you have eyes in your head?"

MA'AM, ARE YOU BIDDING OR POINTING? George says.

Poppy's face reddens. She shakes her head—no, she wasn't bidding. No, no.

"Don't see him," Jim says.

"You're seeing things, Poppy," Ham says. "Probably sun stroke."

She smacks him.

"Ow," he says. "Got me right in the bursitis."

She looks again where the old man was standing. Gone. "You saw him, Mim? Where'd he go?"

"Who?" Mim says.

"He was standing right there a minute ago. You saw him giving us the evil eye."

"I saw no such thing," Mim says. "And neither did Evangeline."


*October 28, 1990*

### SMITH

Broke into Si and Clarabelle's house. With the butt-end of the trowel he'd found by the walk, he smashed a window, knocked out jags of glass. Reached through. Turned the lock. *Shit!* Knicked by a jag he missed. Just a scratch, though his sleeve cut through and would have to be mended. Turned the rattley knob and—easy as that, easy as a bite of Clarabelle's peach pie down the gullet—stepped across the threshold, and he was *in*—after going-on thirty-five years of being *out*!

From deeper inside the house, a rustling. "Who is it? Who's there?" Turned his better ear. Nobody. Nothing.

Then he heard it again—a pattering in the wall; rodents making themselves scarce. He stamped his boot. The rodents made themselves scarcer. A shadow moved by the far door. A silhouette: Si, shotgun in hand. Smith heard, plain as day, the click of the safety. "Hey," he said, raising his hand, as if a hand could stop a spray of pellets or a slug.

Course it wasn't Si at all, but Smith's own shadow, drawn on the wall by the light that followed him in. And the click was only the electric clock marking time.

"Damn fool," he said, "Goddamn fool."

From the bowl of apples on the counter rose a cloud of dust-sized flies. The sweetness of the rotting fruit mixed with the kerosene scent from the heater, but it was as cold inside the house as out. Colder. Even cold, the kitchen smelled the same as it had thirty-five years ago. Pretty much. Looked the same, too; so much so that for an instant he was decades back in time, calling out to the house: "Si. Clarabelle. Boy. Anybody to home?"

Same greasy pine cupboards. Same plaid linoleum, thin underfoot. Same cookstove hulked in the corner, pipe flanged into the chimney, creosote streaking brick. Same creak of floorboards in need of shoring. Except it wasn't the same. Thirty-five years ago, he'd been welcome. But now, not even Dreams End acknowledged him. The mustiness of the old house pushed him back toward the door he'd left open despite the cold. *Out, out, out,* the house seemed to say—like Clarabelle sweeping spiders.

He hadn't wanted to break in. Queasy at the thought as he walked cross-country from his cabin to the homestead. Smith is not usually one to ignore his instincts, but this time he didn't have much choice. Though he knew if Si caught him on his land, in his house for Christ's sake, he probably *would* shoot. Just the excuse the old bastard's been waiting for.

Still, a man could ignore family most of the time, just like they ignored him, but he couldn't ignore duty when life took a turn for the worse, as he was pretty damn sure it had in this house, so quiet he could almost hear the sills rotting, plaster crumbling, chimney shifting. Should have been smoke rising from Si and Clarabelle's chimney this cold, clear morning, but there was none.

Smith lay his hand on the cookstove. Cold. Kerosene heater. Cold. Teakettle empty. Frypan skimmed with rust, as though it had been set out damp after washing. Pot soaking in the sink, scummy water, the remains of what might have been soup. The newspapers hadn't been collected for days, nor the mail.

"Si," he called hoarsely. "Clarabelle." But he knew there would be no answer. "Answer me!" He coughed to clear the place in his throat where the words stuck, walked to the open door, spat in the frosted grass beside the step. The best plan would be to skip out and head home. *What's it to you, Old Man*, he thought, *the thing that's happened in this house?*

Course he couldn't go home, because he knew exactly what it was to him. The moment he crossed the threshold, he'd known. With each step deeper inside, the house pushing at him—*out, out*—he knew. Breaking into Dreams End on this day at this moment, seeing what was there to be seen, doing what needed to be done, this was why he, Smith Forbes, had been born. It was the reason he'd lived so long. And this final family duty was more than likely his only excuse for living still.

That morning Houstiff, the mailman, had caught him by the side of the road where Smith was digging out the leaf-choked culvert. When Houstiff pulled up in his rattletrap Jeep, Smith straightened slowly, climbed out of the ditch, tucked the thick-tined rake under his arm for leaning, stripped off his work gloves. The Jeep's window was down. Through it, Houstiff handed Smith a packet of mail bound with a rubber band. "What do I want with that mess?" Smith said. "Nothing but duns and advertisements."

Houstiff said: "Reason I stopped, Smith . . . reason I stopped: wondering what the story was down the road with your brother and Clarabelle? The house is all closed up like maybe they've gone off. They gone off?"

The engine puttered and pattered, fanning a dust that worked its way up Smith's nose. He drew out his handkerchief and blew.

"Haven't collected their mail out of the box since, I don't know, Monday or Tuesday," Houstiff said. "But nobody told me to hold it, either, so I don't know. Don't know to forward it or hold it or what. The box is full now. Flap's bent—won't close all the way. And a big rain coming, so they say."

"Rain?" Smith said. The sky was cloudless, jewel-blue. "What are you talking about rain?" He tucked the handkerchief deep in his chest pocket. "It's not gonna rain, Houstiff. Look at the goddamn sky. What are you foolish?"

"If Si's mail gets wet, I'm going to hear about it."

Smith shrugged, pulled on his gloves; then, balanced by the rake, stepped down into the ditch like descending stairs.

"Maybe something happened to 'em," Houstiff said. "Maybe something's wrong out there. Do you think?"

"I don't think nothing. They don't tell me nothing." Smith spiraled the rake into the culvert as far as it would go, swished it back and forth until it caught.

Houstiff set right there, never even offered a hand when Smith hauled out a clot of wet leaves and muck along with what was left of a fair-sized animal. The insides had rotted away, but the shape of it remained in the hide and bones.

"Goddamn coon crawled up in and died." Smith turned the carcass with the rake. "Probably had the rabies. They're all dying of the rabies. Come spring there won't be a goddamn coon left in the whole goddamn county." Then: "You had your shots, Houstiff?" Smith raised the bulk of the coon on the flat of the rake and pushed it toward the Jeep. Houstiff pulled his head and arm in quick through the window.

"You better bury that thing up," Houstiff said. "Burn those gloves. Maybe you better call the warden and see what he has to say about it. No sense taking a chance." He revved the engine, jiggled the shift stick. "If you see Si and Clarabelle, tell them I'm holding their mail."

"I don't see 'em," Smith said. "I won't see 'em." He tossed the carcass into the road. There it lay.

*Summers, early 1940s*

### AS KIDS

Mim, Poppy, Ham and Boy swung from the rope—thick as an arm, rough and damp—hanging over the river from a stout limb. Ham pendulumed so high he could double flip before he hit the water, crowing all the way up and all the way down. Boy climbed the rope to the limb itself, balanced on the limb as far out as he dared, dove like a kingfisher, and slid in easily—though he was bigger than all of them, taller and wider through the shoulders and chest, so you'd think he'd make a colossal splash, but no. Even Poppy could tuck, hold her nose, wait for the right moment in the swing, then splat, and bob up like a bottle after.

But when Mim swung on the rope, she'd let go too soon and scrape down the rocky banking. (Her knees still show the scars.) Or she wouldn't let go at all and end up pendulum weight, the others yelling "Jump!", Mim refusing, holding on for dear life, her face pressed to the hemp, losing her grip in the long, humiliating, inevitable slide, a performance so arresting Poppy forgot to tread water and got a snout full. Boy turned his eyes away in empathy, and even wicked Cousin Ham offered no comment but laughter.

*Always*

### GRAMMIE OLD

Anticipated bad news, bad luck, and tragedy in dreams that came to her most times when she was sleeping, but sometimes when she was awake with that faraway look clouding her eyes. It's the Irish in you, the aunties said, all named Moynihan and from the old country. "A penny for your thoughts," her mother would say. But Grammie, even as a child, knew her thoughts were worth more than that.

"What are you looking at?" the grandchildren and great-grand-children would ask, when she grew as old as the aunties had been.

"Nothing," she'd say. "Just looking."

Some said tragedy had made her senses more acute than normal people's. But she didn't acknowledge either the tragedy or the gift. She believed in living on, living through, as you are. Took comfort from an old soul in the eyes of a newborn. When she declared, "This little one has his grampa in him," she meant it. She refused to believe her luck was any worse than the next person's or that the Forbes family had been or would be any harder hit by accident and illness than any other. Death was part of life. People you loved died and that was that, especially if you lived to be a hundred, or close to.

Some say Grammie Old haunts Dreams End, conjuring in the shadows. Some say she manifests not as an old woman but middle-aged, in a dark dress under a faded apron pinned at the shoulders. They say she floats a few inches above the ground (either that or she's grown tall), her abundant hair fluffed like dandelion gone to seed, as if you could blow it away, and her, too, with a single breath.

Mim saw her once by the river at dusk—barefoot, wading. She seemed off-balance, awkward in the long dress hiked up to her knees. She was smiling as though she knew how funny she looked. Mim smiled back. She blinked. Grammie was gone. Mim thought maybe it was time to invest in a new pair of glasses.

Clarabelle used to see ghosts quite often—some she recognized, some she didn't—four or five times a year anyway. Course Clara-belle lived right there at the house and had more opportunity. "They never have much to say," Clarabelle observed. "Soon as they hear Si or anybody moving around in the other room, they go."

As strong a presence in death as in life, they say, Grammie Old and the others are as much a part of Dreams End as the wavy glass in the six-over-nine windows, the seven layers of paint on the pantry floor, the gunstock corner beams.

They are right.

*Warm weather, late '30s and '40s*

### BOY

Loved hornpouting. Pout don't get hungry until after dark, so he and his father and Uncle Smith would row out at dusk and wait until the pout showed an interest in lively crawlers fresh dug from Grammie Old's mulch heap. Wouldn't even need to bait a whole crawler once the pout started biting good, an inch or two would do. Course the crawlers weren't so lively after they'd been cut up.

Plop the catch into bucket to thrash until they exhausted themselves. That was best—to let them die on their own, in their own time, rather than snap the spine like you might with a trout. Cuts from pout horns went deep and were a long time healing, witness the scar curved a like new moon in the flesh of his palm.

Boy loved fishing Small Pond with his father and Uncle Smith. On clear nights, stars shone twice—in the sky and in the water. Twin stars. Twin moons. His father and Smith were twins, too! Full moon, they fished without the lantern, moon shadows casting over the water: Si in the bow, Smith in the stern, Boy in the middle. A shadow is like a twin. Boy pretended his shadow was his twin. They wore their lucky fishing hats and rested the grips of their spinning rods across their knees.

Other nights, when the moon was small or clouded over, Uncle Smith lit the lantern and set it on the middle seat beside Boy. "Don't knock it overboard," Smith said, "or we'll be stuck out here till morning." Which wasn't true, because the darkness was never complete, not even on the cloudiest of cloudy nights. After their eyes adjusted, they'd be able to find their way. Course they would.

Once he had accidentally knocked the lantern overboard—clipped it with his elbow, and when he tried to grab hold, knocked it over the side instead. "Oh no," he said, watching the light sink. It stayed lit a long time under the water. "Jesus H. Christ," his father said. "Can't you sit still a minute. Now look what you gone and done."

"It was my lantern," Smith said, "and I don't give a shit. Got another one just like it to home."

They had to stop pouting then, because they couldn't see to thread the crawlers on the hooks, but they found their way to the landing just fine. It wasn't far to shore, and the land was darker than the water, like a black line on black paper. Now Boy is careful not to brush against the lantern even lightly. He keeps a distance between himself and it, sits right still.

The lantern spreads a glow over the boat and water, a steady flame, sooty glass. His father's face is all angles with eyes like daubs of paint. His uncle looks the same. Si in the bow, Smith in the stern, Boy in the middle. The boat anchored at both ends so it won't turn and tangle the lines. They fish for hours, fill the bucket. The pout thrash a lot at first, then not so often, then not at all. Once a pout stops thrashing you pick it out—use the glove so the horns don't slice you—cut off its head, clean it, skin it, throw the skin and guts in the pond for chum. They keep a tally of who catches the most and the biggest. They weigh the big ones on the spring-and-hook scale and measure them with the stick. Sometimes Boy takes the prize. Sometimes Si. Sometimes Smith. At the end, Smith writes the date and the catch on the gunnel in very small numbers to leave room the next night and the next.

Next day, Boy's mother fries the pout in bacon fat and corn meal. Smith comes over. They eat pout and greens. Boy sucks the flaky white meat off the big bones and avoids the feathery ones that can stick in your throat and choke you to death. He is careful not to swallow any bones he feels scratching the roof of his mouth or piercing his gums. He works the bones forward, extricates them with a napkin. Si and Smith pick bones out of their mouths with their fingers. Sometimes they spit them into their plates. This isn't polite, but his mother says pay no attention—teaching those two manners is a hopeless cause.

"I raised those boys to have manners," Grammie says. "I guess they misplaced them somewhere along the way." She made sour cherry cobbler for dessert.

"No one's blaming you," Boy's mother says. "Put a platter of pout in front of them, they revert!"

Si sits at one end of the table, Smith at the other, Boy and Grammie Old on one side, Boy's mother across.

"This little one is especially tasty," Grammie says. "Did you catch it, Boy?"

He inspects what's left of the fish on her plate. "Maybe."

"I bet you did," she says. "It tastes like you caught it."

In the yellow light of the kitchen, Si and Smith look more alike than usual—especially their eyes, an identical dusky-blue. Later, in his room, undressed for bed, Boy studies his face in the mirror for signs of the whiskers he hopes are beginning to sprout. No whiskers, but when he looks into his own eyes he is startled by their color—that same dusky-blue, but brightened with surprise.


*March 1901*

### GRAMMIE OLD

Saw death coming down the road a long way off. Sometimes it fooled her, took a detour, and never made it to the house. Not usually. Usually when she saw death coming, it came, and in short order, too. Two nights before Martin drowned, she dreamed the well was dry and alive with swallows flying in and out like bees at a hive. She woke with a skipping heart, but kept her premonition to herself, because she knew better than anyone that what is meant to be almost certainly will. No sense getting everybody worked up.

She took to her bed the next day with a headache. Martin took the horses and the sledge onto Small Pond to harvest ice with her brother Eff and men from town. But the ice off the landing, thinned by a freak current, couldn't support the weight and the whole business fell through: horses, sledge, and Martin himself, weighed down with boots, wool pants, long underwear, and a sheepskin jacket.

Still, they say he could have pulled himself out on the stout rope the others secured to a tree and tossed from the safety of good ice. Eff later told how Martin, instead of saving himself, waved the others back and dove to free the horses. Eff said Martin came up once for air, then down again. This time he stayed down so long that the surface stilled; the broken ice stopped bobbing.

Somebody said: "They're gone."

Somebody else said: "Can't be. Ain't that deep."

Pretty soon the heads and shoulders of the horses broke the surface, water fountaining out of their huffing nostrils as they crashed a channel toward shore.

Some ran to intercept them. Others kept watching for Martin, thinking he'd be right along, too. Eff thought for sure Martin would be hanging off a horse's tail, skimming along, and just a-grinning. He thought any second Martin would poke up through like Jacksprung-from-the-box. Thought he'd grab hold, and they'd haul him sputtering in, hoist him onto the good ice and steer him to shore, slap him on the back, wrap him in coats and take him home to warm up.

Which might very well have happened except Grammie Old, young then and known as Julia, dreamed of swallows. "If I hadn't believed he'd be fine, Julia, I'd have gone in after him," Eff said. "Thing was, the pond wasn't even hardly deep where the horses fell through, just seven feet or ten. Not hardly deep enough for a man to drown, not Martin anyway." Maybe the water chilled him to the bone before he even realized. Maybe, in the scramble to free the horses, he'd been knocked out by a flailing hoof—though, three hours later, when they dredged him up, they saw no marks or bruises. Why hadn't somebody gone in after him right then? All those men standing there, looking on. Why hadn't somebody . . . ?

But when one didn't go, the others didn't either: each waiting for the other, each thinking the other knew what was best, and all of them believing Martin would any second pop up out of that black water just-a-grinning. Truth was, if somebody had gone in after him, there might well have been two drowned men instead of one, or five, or seven; two widows or five or seven; and a dozen more fatherless children. The rope had been the best bet, and Martin was strong, the strongest among them. "He could have saved himself and let the horses go," Eff said. Then, after another whiskey: "By God, he should have."

Somebody said get the horses back to the barn before they caught pneumonia. Somebody said get 'em inside and rub 'em down. Somebody said, "They're already headed." Somebody said, "Jesus, where is Martin?"

Maybe he tangled in the harness, or his clothes caught a root, or his foot wedged under the sledge or between rocks—though three hours later, when they dredged him out, he came easy enough, tangled in nothing, not even a pond weed. Eff said, after another whiskey, the whole thing seemed like a dream they dreamed together. Dreaming awake, Julia called it, the gift (or curse) of the Moynihans back many generations. By the time the truth dawned that Martin was gone, by the time the men realized he wasn't going to emerge from that cold black water on his own, it was as if they were all saying to each other (but not out loud): Wake up, fellas, wake up for God's sake! It's morning. We're alive. The sun's out and shining off the ice so bright it hurts to look. Martin Forbes can't die before us all on a morning like this. No one dies in the open air on a morning like this. It's not possible.

Course it was.

Nobody woke up. They tried but couldn't. And who the hell was going to break the news to Julia? Course nobody had to. She knew. She'd dreamed her husband's death in swallows two nights before. "He couldn't have stood to let those sweet bay horses drown harnessed to the sledge," she said.

"A fine pair," Eff said. "A fine matched pair of workers."

"You have them," Julia said. "I've no use for them. They belong to you now."

Instead of a gift, the offer felt to Eff something like a curse, though he knew she didn't intend it that way.

Smith and Si were nine years old when their father drowned. They watched, hidden among the shoreline spruce, as the body was pulled from the water. Forbidden to leave the house, and no-body told them why, they sneaked out and watched as the men dragged somebody's flat-bottom scow to the little bit of open water and floated it. From the scow, two men dragged the bottom with a hook. A third chiseled the ice closing in around them. Hours passed. When the hook finally caught, they pulled the body to the surface hand-over-hand, and a row of men on shore pulled the scow hand-over-hand on long ropes from open water, through thin ice, onto good ice, all the way in—the body dragging behind like a big fish, fresh caught—one bare hand and wrist flopping along the ice like a separate thing.

Eff tucked a blanket around the body and three men (one held the head, one the middle, one the feet) lay it heavily in the wagon like putting a drunk to bed. Eff crouched beside the soggy bundle, head to his knees, as the wagon jogged toward home, pulled not by the bays but by somebody else's horse, shaggy and black with a crooked white stripe down her nose—a horse Smith and Si had never seen before and never saw after. The boys followed at a dis-tance, running in and out of the trees, ducking behind stone walls. The snow was frozen and only an inch or two deep. The ground was frozen, too. Every step crunched, but nobody looked back. The men walking beside the wagon kept their heads down, like Eff, like the driver—as though they were too weak to hold them up. They let the horse lead the way.

The boys sneaked back into the house the same way they'd sneaked out. They climbed the back stairs to their room and sat side-by-side on the bed, their backs stiff against the headboard. Maybe they fell asleep that way, eyes open; maybe they were dreaming awake. That's how their mother found them some time later, when she gathered the children—the twins, little Lucretia, and the baby, Hamilton, just two years old—to tell them what had happened—that their father was dead and would be buried on Sunday.

No one but Smith and Si themselves ever knew what they'd wit-nessed that day at Small Pond, or how it made them feel. They never never spoke of it, not even to each other.

*October 1990*

## CLARABELLE

Died first, they said, of heart failure. Not an attack exactly, more like the sputtering out of a worn pump. Probably in her sleep, though it was hard to tell so long after the fact. Probably went to bed as usual. Tucked up. Blackberry tea with honey in a bone-colored mug on her bedside table. She went to bed with her tea and her book, fell asleep, and didn't wake up. Crossed over, as Grammie Old would have said, unknowing. Oblivious. Would Clarabelle's ghost even realize she was one?

The morning after she died, Si must have been up early, as usual, rattling around. He fires up the wood stove, collects the paper from the box, eats his toast, drinks instant coffee, fills the bird feeder, splits fresh kindling, sweeps leaves off the porch.

Midmorning. Still no Clarabelle. Not a peep out of her.

Maybe he looks in on her, cracks the door and sticks his head through. Maybe he calls to her, steps uneasily to her bedside. Bends over her, touches hand, arm, shoulder, eyelid. Maybe he feels a wash of affection, wants to crawl in beside her and gather her up. Maybe he is shocked. Bewildered. Horrified. Grief-stricken. Maybe he's afraid. Or . . . is it possible, even likely, he never checked in on her at all? Simply went about his business and let her, as usual, go about hers?

Either way, he left her to rest, at rest, upstairs undisturbed, in the four-poster bed they'd stopped sharing long ago—during the bleak months after they lost Boy. Still and always fond and familiar, but unable to look at one another, because when they did, they saw their son, or an echo of him, hovering just there (or there) like air bent into visibility by the heat of the wood stove.

Maybe at first Si thought she really was sleeping.

Each morning, for seven or ten mornings afterwards, he fires up the wood stove, collects the paper, eats his toast, drinks his coffee, splits fresh kindling, collects the mail, fills the feeder, sweeps the porch. He does morning chores, afternoon chores; works a jigsaw puzzle, watches television; writes checks for the bills that come in, mails them off.

He could have called the doctor, the police, the funeral home. Could have contacted someone from the family, maybe Barbara. Could have buried her himself in a corner of his beautiful hayfield. But he didn't. There she lay a week or more, they speculated, before he succumbed himself. She had died of heart failure; he died when a blood vessel burst in his head. Probably didn't feel it coming on any more than she had. Or maybe he did.

She was probably asleep when her time came (or ran out—depending on how you looked at it); he was probably awake. Maybe for him the crossing over began as a headache. Or a dizzy spell. A nightmare. Or a vision. Maybe he knew. Maybe he willed it. Welcomed it.

*August 24, 1991*

### HENRY

Raises a thirty-five-gallon crock with flow-blue stenciling. Hoists it to his shoulder to show it off, then lowers it to nestle against his belt buckle.

"Bid on that, Lucy, why don't you?" Barbara says. "Make pickles."

"I'll let you," Lucy says. "Here—hand over your card—I'll bid for you if you're too shy. What's your number?"

"Keep your hands off my card, Lucy."

Hands in her baby's armpits, fingers circling his chest, Lucy holds the squirming redhead out to her cousin. Barbara makes no move to take him. The baby hangs in the air.

"Don't be dangling him like that, Lucy," Poppy says, "You're going to pop his little arms right out of their sockets."

"She's not popping sockets, Poppy," Mim says. "Look how contented." Evangeline agrees.

"Come to Gramma." Poppy reaches for the baby. "Sit with me,

now. Stay with me." She jiggles him. The baby tries to eat the buttons on her blouse.

"God, Barbara." Lucy's wiry hair tickles Barbara's cheek. "How many more chances do you think you're going to get? Young, good-looking, an artist. With money. And he wasn't boring. You can put up with a lot if they're not boring. It counts for a lot. And he adored you."

"That's debatable."

"God Barbara, you're pushing forty." She's not. Not even close. "Were you a bitch to him? You can be such a bitch."

Henry lifts the crock's clay lid to display the interior. A mouse flies out into the front row. Lands on Houstiff's neck, but doesn't linger. Houstiff jumps up, "What the hey!" A woman claps her hand to her heart. Henry drops the crock, which bounces, but miraculously doesn't break. A stringy nest lands on his boot. He kicks it off. "Yikes," he says. "Inhabited."

Grenadine grabs Barbara's shoulder and squeezes.

"Ow," Barbara says.

"Vermin," Grenadine wails. "Where'd it go? Could be anywhere?"

Barbara agrees that this is so.

FIFTY-DOLLARS-FOR-THIS-FINE-OLD-CROCKERY FIFTY-FIF-TY-FIFTY- FORTY-WHERE? PAY ATTENTION FOLKS. MICE NOT IN-CLUDED. OR IF YOU WANT 'EM, MAYBE WE CAN ROUND 'EM UP. WHAT DO YOU SAY, HENRY? WHO'LL-SAY-THIRTY-AND-GO . . .

"I can't get over it," Lucy says. "You and Brad—I thought for sure—"

"Get over it," Barbara says.

ARE YOU ALL DONE AT THIRTY-FIVE? IT'S OLD. IT'S GOOD.

"You ought to bid on the cradle, Lucy," Barbara says. "Coming up next. Go ahead. You know you want to."

"This guy's already too big for a cradle, aren't you? You're a big guy, huh? Like your daddy."

"Bid on it, Lucy," Poppy says. "It's a heirloom."

"You bid, Mumma."

"Not me," Poppy says. "You bid, Mim. You can put your dolls in it."

"I don't keep my dolls. I give them away."

"You never gave me one," Poppy says.

"Do you want one?"

"I'd take one."

"Oh no!" Evangeline says. "Not me."

Mim strokes her rag-wool hair.

TWO-WHERE AND-NOW-THE-THREE AND THREE-FIFTY-FOUR . . .

"My goodness," Grenadine says. "That's quite a lot for that thing. Why it's falling apart, practically."

"It's old. It's primitive," says the pewter-haired dealer who smells like the sea.

AND-FOUR-FIFTY- FIVE-HUNDRED-WHERE?

"What did you do to the poor man, Barbara?" Lucy says. "Did you stifle his creativity?"

"Yes," Barbara says, "I stifled it."

"I might bid on those old toys," Lucy says. "Maybe the choo-choo. See the choo-choo. You'd like a choo-choo," to the baby.

"You'd think *somebody* would have checked the crockery for mice," Poppy says. "You'd think George and his crew could have cleaned some of this stuff up. Look how black that cradle is—probably an entirely different color under all that grime. People don't even know what they're buying."

"You'd think somebody might have at least taken a cloth and wiped things over," Grenadine says. "I'd have been glad to but nobody asked me."

The pewter-haired dealer says: "That's authentic eighteenth-century dirt, complete with mites. Tories, probably. Pin them under a microscope, check out their wigs and Union Jacks."

"If there was damage," Poppy says, "you'd never spot it till you got it home and washed it up with Lestoil. I think George left some of these things dirty on purpose to hide the bungs."

The baby reaches for the strap of Barbara's pocketbook, latches on.

"The more they pay for that dirty old stuff, Mumma," Lucy says, "the bigger your cut."

The baby pulls hard on the strap. "Ow," Barbara says, and pulls back. The strap slides from the baby fist. "Ha!" she says, but he's still reaching, horizontal from Lucy's hip, like a caterpillar groping for its next hold. Lucy shifts him to the other hip.

"That old Victrola," Barbara says, "in front of the jelly cupboard. You can just see the top of it from here. Where'd that come from? Poppy, Mim, do you know? I don't remember seeing it in the house."

"Probably the attic," Poppy says. "You wouldn't believe the stuff they brought out of that attic. Old old dusty dirty. You couldn't even walk around up there. Couldn't even crawl through some places. Nobody in this family ever threw a thing away, just lugged it up to the attic and forgot about it."

"What Victrola?" Grenadine says.

"You ought to have it," Barbara says. "It'd look nice in the dining room, next to that maple hutch. It'd go perfectly with that piss pot candy dish."

"What kind of candy dish?" Lucy says.

"She's being funny," Grenadine says. "Barbara's making a little joke."

"Why don't you go look it over—the Victrola—see if it's something you're interested in," Barbara says. "Wind it up. Make sure the turntable turns. They'll let you."

"Tell them you're family," Lucy suggests.

The baby fusses. To shut him up, Lucy offers one of her earrings, a silver clip-on big as a grape. He takes it into his mouth, sucks vigorously.

"He'll choke!" Poppy says.

"He won't choke, Mumma. It feels good on his gums. He knows not to swallow."

Poppy's out of her chair. Sticks a finger in the baby's mouth and extricates the earring, slides back into her chair, tucks the earring in her pocket. Lucy glares at the top of her mother's head, gray curls tight as macaroni in the box. The baby fusses. Lucy pulls off her other earring, pokes it in his mouth. He's happy. They are all happy for the moment.

*November 3, 1990*

### SMITH

Told the whole story just once to Barbara who drove all the way from Portsmouth to hear it and show her face at Si and Clarabelle's graveside funeral while she was in the vicinity. She tried to get Smith to show his face too; said people would expect it. But he didn't think he'd be welcome. "Who?" she said. "Who are you worried about? Not my father, or Mim or Poppy or Lucy. Not anybody from the village—if anybody shows."

"They'll be there," he said. "They'll all be there."

The two sat side-by-side on the hand-hewn steps of Smith's cabin. It was mid-day, warm, warming. Indian summer. Smith said, "They day I found Si and Clarabelle, it was cold. Real cold. Colder than it had been; colder than it was going to be. Cold morning, but no smoke from the chimney, Barbara. And that upstairs window wide open. Papers stuffed tight in the box. And the mail piled up. Pounded the front door, back door, side door—loud enough to wake the dead."

"Not quite."

"When the old bastard didn't shoot me, I knew it would be bad. Smashed a window, reached in careful so I wouldn't cut myself— but I did anyway, goddamn fool—turned the lock, let myself in. Jesus." He scrutinized the road in front of the cabin—a stretch of gravel just visible through the thicket of hemlock he cultivates as a hedge. He watched the road, listening hard, as though expecting traffic. There was no traffic. There would be none. Dead end. Used to go somewhere. Not anymore.

"Barbara," he said. "I've been in some *situations* in my time. Been some places I didn't want to be, faced down fellas I didn't want anything to do with, seen things I didn't want to see, done things I didn't want to do—and some I shouldn't have. But walking into the house that day—Jesus, I wanted to turn right around, head home."

"Why didn't you? Anybody else would have. I would have."

"I don't believe it," he said. "Don't believe you would have." Then he started in on how goddamn Houstiff stopped off, informed him Si and Clarabelle hadn't taken in their mail for some days and rain coming on: did Smith know where they'd got to?

"Where the hell did he think they got to, Barbara? The old truck set right there in the barn. How far did he think those two old birds would've got on foot—Clarabelle all hunched over with brittle bones, and Si with his two bum knees. Did Houstiff think they hiked up the back side of Forbes Mountain to take in the view? Did he think they run fifteen miles to Bristol to catch a goddamn bus? You'd think after a day—after *one* day they didn't take in the mail—he'd know something was up."

"You'd think so," she said.

"Except Houstiff don't know nothing. Never has."

"Locked up tighter'n a drum the house was," he said. "Except for the one window upstairs. Which was another thing out of kilter: that window like one eye open, curtains flapping in the breeze. Well, there wa'n't a breeze, but if there had been, they woulda flapped. And the rest of the house all buttoned up. Tried every door, even the bulkhead—buttoned right up like they'd left town. Like they'd took a long trip, which a-course they had."

"Jesus," she said.

"Broke in. Had to. Broke a window in the kitchen door. Goddamn, it was quiet in that house. Empty. Never been in a place so goddamned empty as that house that day. Pot soaking in the sink. Apples rotten on the table. Found him in the living room, setting in his big recliner chair, reclined. There he sat, Barbara; eyes wide open. And Christ if he didn't look just like me!"

"You would have seen me whipping out of that house so fast," she said. "I would've screamed. I would have run. They'd have heard me screaming in Bristol."

"Television was on," he said. "That was some weird. Television was on but the sound turned down—no sound, just picture. Some game show. They were giving away a Christly boat, and girls in bathing suits draped all over it. There sits my brother Si, staring at the screen, enjoying the show, I guess. First thing, I shut off the goddamn TV. Then I got right in that old man's face, looked him straight in his two dead eyes, and I said to him, 'You sit right there, you sorry old bastard. You sit right still for once in your life and listen to me one time.' He sat right there."

"He would," Barbara said. She was crying. She was smiling and crying. She put her head to her knees and locked her hands over it. She was shaking. She was shaking and laughing and crying, but she wasn't making any noise.

"'Si Forbes,' I told him, 'I got nothing to be sorry for. I know it; so do you. But, you know what—no you don't know, so I'm going to tell you—I'm sorry anyway. I'm sorry these last thirty-odd years had to be the way they had to be. And I'm sorry there wa'n't nothing neither you nor I nor anybody else in this world could do about it. You hear me you stubborn old bastard. You hear me Si Forbes, goddamn you all to hell.' He didn't say nothing."

Barbara lifted her head: "He wouldn't."

"But he heard me all right. The old bastard heard me."

"Jesus." Her face was wet. Soaked.

"Him, too."


*January 5, 1960*

### DREAMING AWAKE

Is like living a dream. Not like day or night dreaming, it's like being in two places at once. In your head and not in your head. Like having two bodies. A real body and a dream one—except when you're dreaming awake you can't tell one from the other. It can make you dizzy if you're not used to it, like when Boy and the cousins played the spinning game—twirling in the meadow with their arms spread wide, bumping each other, whirling and falling, forgetting which way was up.

When Boy dreams awake, he goes away but he always comes back.

"Where the hell does he go, Clarabelle?" His father's voice splinters. "Where the hell? Why the hell?" He studies Boy's eyes, as if Boy is holding out. Boy doesn't know what to say.

"He comes back, Si," his mother says. "That's the main thing."

"It's not *you* he's mad at," she tells Boy.

But Boy knows, sure as he knows apple-wood from oak, that it is.

He loves his father as much as he loves the woods; the work; the tree scent as the crosscut butters through a crust of bark and new growth toward center where the wood resists: older, tougher. Bright January day. Boy pulls one way on the bendy, long-toothed saw slicing the trunk of the red oak, a line tree, dying. Smith pulls the other way. Wood dust thickens the air, settles out at their feet. Chip-dog torments squirrels along the stone wall.

"Chip-dog," Smith says, "you ain't gonna catch no goddamn squirrel. You never caught one yet and you ain't going to catch one today."

"He's got one cornered," Boy says.

"He ain't," Smith says. "It run out the other side of the wall. Saw it go."

Chip-dog digs; clods fly and his nose crusts. He pokes the crater he's made in the frozen mat of leaves and pine needles where the squirrel disappeared, certain the squirrel is just inches away, out of sight but not out of smell. Chip-dog doesn't know the squirrel has moved on and left only his scent behind.

"Squirrel's gone," Boy says. "All gone, Chip-dog."

The dog whines, snuffles.

Boy pulls one way. Smith pulls the other. The saw finds its own way in—like wire through a wheel of cheese—traveling through growth rings into the year before and the year before that, then ten years back, twenty-five, thirty-three, thirty-four. Back to the year

Boy was born: the month, the day, the minute. He feels the touch of the blade at the moment of his birth, as though he is the one being cut. He expects blood. Checks for it on his shirt, pants, boots.

Smith pulls one way. Boy pulls the other. Chip-dog has run off. They hear him barking at something he thinks he's treed between them and the state road. "Chip-dog," Smith calls. "Get your hairy ass back here!" Boy whistles, but the dog pays no attention. They hear him barking wildly, then steadily, as though he'll never stop.

Suddenly, he does.

"Either he got the critter or the critter got him," Smith says.

Boy says, "He gave up. Or the critter got away. He'll be all right." But he worries. Dogs get hit in the road sometimes, or shot by hunters who can't tell a dog from a deer, or choose not to.

"Course he'll be all right," Smith says. "He always comes back. Eventually. Couldn't get rid of the little bastard if I tried. And I've tried."

As they work the tree, Boy listens for barking far off, for a four-footed rush through the undergrowth, for the jangle of snaps on a leather collar. But he hears no dog sounds, not even when he and Smith pause for a breather. Must have headed out the other way— maybe on to the state road; maybe, Boy hopes, toward home.

"He'll be all right," Boy says.

"Sure he will," Smith says.

They are making good progress. Si will be impressed when he returns from the mill. The tree groans. The saw catches. Smith frees it with a wedge and four strikes of the maul. Sawdust and chips cling to their boots and their socks, pant legs. Boy tries not to think about Chip-dog lost or hurt. Back and forth, give and take, sluice and slice, the saw finds the way to that dark, soft, barely imaginable time before Boy was even born. Trying to imagine it is like rolling down a spongy mountain wrapped in a blanket. At the base, when he rolls at last to a stop, he lies still as a length of pipe, breathing his own breath. After a while, he opens his eyes; can't see through the blanket tucked close over his face. That's all right, because outside it is just as dark, maybe darker. Feels tears coming, but he isn't sad. The damp reminds him he's alive. He wonders after a while—a second, an eternity—if he is really there at all. Wonders if he is really anywhere. Wonders if he really is.

Before he was born the trees were here. But smaller. All the people older than him were here, too. But younger. And the boulder he sat on to eat his lunch. And the stripe of milk-quartz like petrified lightning across its flat face. A crack that isn't. As if the rock were an ancient egg. And, inside . . . who knows? Maybe another world. Maybe another Boy on another rock eating his same lunch of corned beef and sharp cheese.

Before he was born the ground was solid beneath the leaves that fell this year and the one before and so on until you're so far back the leaves are soil, black under your nails, crumbly in your hand. And if you dig even farther, the soil grows richer, blacker, purified, as though it's not dirt or dirty at all, and veined with pale roots fine as the thread Grammie Old guides though the invisible eye of an invisible needle. And the icy brook tumbles into the river skimmed with cold-snap ice during a freeze-and-thaw winter like this one but a hundred years ago. Or five hundred. Or a thousand. Or forever.

*1936*

### AUNT LUCRETIA

Played the piano. Closed her eyes and tipped her head so her hair— thick and smooth as tar—draped her back and you could see the soft under her chin. Her fingers spidered the keys, and the music rose as if it were in her hands instead of the instrument, as if when she curled her hands a certain way, when she pressed her finger tips just so on the ivory, the music oozed out like sap from a sugar maple. Boy knew Lucretia's touch was special, because when he pressed those same keys, there was no music (except in his head) only noise.

When the cousins used to gather, usually at Dreams End, but sometimes at Mim and Lucretia's, Boy would try to play and the cousins would make faces behind his back. He saw them reflected in the polish of piano wood. Mim's teeth denting her lower lip.

Ham's face twisted like a rung-out rag. Poppy's hands pressed over her mouth, her shoulders twitching until laughter, finally, spat out between her fingers. "It's a funny song," she said. "Isn't it supposed to be a funny song?"

"I never heard *that* song before," Ham said. "I never heard anything like it. What do you call it, 'Squawking Chickens Chased by a Pack of Wild Dogs'?"

Mim said: "There's nothing wrong with that song. It's as good as you could do, Ham! A perfectly fine song. I like it." But Boy knew she didn't really. She just didn't like to hurt his feelings.

Ham said, "It ought to be on the radio," and punched Boy between the shoulder blades. Then he punched his sister in the arm—not hard—but Poppy wailed. Then he tackled Mim and wrestled her onto the cushions of Aunt Lucretia's velvety couch. Mim squealed, flipped him, smothered him with a cross-stitch pillow until he cried, "Mercy!" Boy was laughing now because Ham's legs flailed and one sock had fallen down revealing a white, bony ankle.

Poppy said: "You're going to break something, you two. You broke my arm, Ham. Look, I'm getting a black and blue. I'm telling Mumma." Ham punched her on the other arm.

Mim said: "My house; my turn," and squeezed Boy off the piano bench. He sprawled on the couch with Ham. Poppy collapsed on the floor: "I'm telling."

"I'm telling, too," Ham said.

Mim played "Santa Lucia" from the book with the fancy cover called Old-Fashioned Favorites. "Now 'neath the silver moon, ocean is glow-o-ing," her singing voice higher and tremblier than her talking voice. Boy let his head hang off the couch, felt the rush of blood to his brain. The cushions were so firm and smooth he couldn't help sliding toward the floor and had to lock his heels over the back to hold his place. He sang—softly, just to himself—what words he could remember from the song he'd heard so many times. He closed his eyes, saw the billowing waves, the round moon, the moving shadows.

Mim picked out the tune with two hands. Testing for wrong

notes. She knew to sit straight, curl her fingers as though she were holding two balls, move her hands one way when the black marks went down on the page, and the other way when they went up. The more flags on the notes, the faster you played them. Lucretia had taught her that, and Mim tried to teach Boy. But the notes refused to stay still long enough for him to know their order. And it seemed like the harder he looked, the faster they danced off the page, up the wall, across the ceiling, down the other wall, out the window.

Besides, the truth was neither he nor Mim had the gift of making real music like Lucretia—music that tingled your skin, lit pictures in your head, and squeezed your heart. And the hard truth was, they never would.

*May 1990*

## JIM

And Si were at the drop-leaf table drinking coffee, eating biscuits with jelly, looking out the window, not talking much, when they spotted Smith hiking down the road. At the time Jim didn't know it was Smith. Had no idea who it was. An old man walking along— Jim wondered who he might be, where he might be going since the road dead-ended not far beyond the house. Thought he might be a neighbor stopping by.

Si's reaction puzzled him. The old man half-stood, leaned across the table until his face nearly touched the window glass, said something Jim couldn't make out. Slapped the table so hard the coffee cups jumped. So did Jim.

"Woah," Jim said, "that's hot," and wiped coffee from his wrist with a towel. He'd been eating a biscuit, nearly choked. Wondered where Poppy and Clarabelle had got to, wished they'd come back, around somewhere—looking at something, for something—he hadn't paid much attention when they wandered off, leaving him and Si to get acquainted. This was the weekend Poppy had chosen to show off her new husband to the relatives. Jim didn't mind. He liked Yankees. And biscuits, too.

The old man on the road kept coming. Pretty soon he was close enough for Jim to get a good look and do a double take, because the old man on the road and the one at the table looked enough alike to be twins. Turned out they were. Si didn't say so, but Poppy explained the situation later on the drive home. Twin brothers and they hadn't spoken for years.

"I figured something was up," Jim said.

"They were close all their lives," Poppy told him. "Smith and Si did everything together since they were kids, hunting, fishing, a little farming. They were in the wood business together for years and made pretty good money at it, too. Then Boy died—and that was the end of that. No one says, no one *will* say, because that's how this family is, but all of a sudden you can't mention Smith to Si nor Si to Smith. And you take a chance mentioning Boy's name to either one. It's hard on the family, especially Clarabelle. Ridiculous—holding a grudge like that. Forbes-stubborn, Clarabelle says. But those two are stubborner than all the rest of us put together."

Smith had stood for a long time at the end of the driveway. At first it seemed like he was going to turn in, walk right up to the front door maybe, sit with them at the table for coffee and biscuit. But no. He just stood there.

"Doing his statue act," Poppy said.

"Whatever it was, Old Si didn't like it." He'd watched Smith for a minute or five; Smith standing at the foot of the driveway as though he'd forgotten where he was or where he'd intended to go. "Son-of-a-bitch," Si said, and drew a shotgun from the long shadow between the table and the woodbox. Checked the load, lay the gun across the table—barrel angled toward the window. "If that bastard takes one step in this direction, one step off the public road and onto my goddamn property, I will shoot him."

Jim laughed. Thought he was supposed to. "Beautiful grain on that stock," he said. "What is it, walnut?"

"And he damn well knows it, too. Damn well better. Look at him. Son-of-a-bitch couldn't move any slower if he tried." Smith edged by the end of the driveway, past the mailbox, down the middle of the road toward the bar gap. He appeared deep in thought.

"He don't need to walk by this house to get to the river or the pond or the village or wherever the hell he thinks he's going. No need to be walking by this house. Only reason he walks by this goddamn house is to get my goddamn goat, that's why."

Down at the road, turned around now, heading back, Smith's gait was slow and particular, as though each step were a chore, as though after each step he pondered whether to take another. Jim ate a second biscuit. At the point where Smith came closest to the house, Jim could see him clearly and in profile—the long nose, square jaw, wattled neck peppered with a fresh growth of silver beard. Just like Si. Denim overalls, collarless button front shirt, fastened high on the neck. Railroad cap. In younger days, the twins had both worked on the railroad. Still wore the caps. Smith's was on his head. Si's hung from a peg by the door.

"If that bastard so much as looks this way . . ." Si said. "If he so much as turns his goddamn head in this direction . . ."

But Smith didn't turn his goddamn head. He just kept walking.

*Late October, early November 1990*

## SOME

Called it husbandly devotion, some a touch of Alzheimer's, or hardening of the arteries. Some called it crazy. Why hadn't Si gotten help as soon as he realized Clarabelle had passed away? What on God's good earth was he thinking, leaving her lay up there all that time without a proper burial? Clarabelle would have wanted a proper, timely burial. Course she would. Who wouldn't? She'd have been mortified if she'd realized he left her lay up there, wrapped in a ratty old quilt all that time. Jimmy Crost from the Rescue Squad said it was quite a sight—Si and Clarabelle locked together in that creepy old house, chock full of stuff, wall to wall, floor to ceiling, cellar to attic stuff. And chock full of ghosts, too, some said. You couldn't see them, but you knew they were there.

Si opened the window to keep her cool. And it stayed cold, unseasonably cold. Still, after a week or two . . .

Some said it was stubbornness, plain and simple. Si's business was his business, and nobody else's. Clarabelle was dead, he was dying, and it was nobody's business but their own. The one thing Si Forbes couldn't stand was pity. But wasn't it an awful thing, cruel and crazy, to leave her lay. To open the window, lock the doors, sit himself in his recliner chair, and die. After a fashion.

Good thing Si and Clarabelle didn't have cats, they said. Down to Soucook some old guy died at home, nobody found him for a week or three. He had a lot of cats. They ate all the food in the house, then started in on him. Said so in the paper. You couldn't really blame the cats.

But in the end, Clarabelle proved her own stubbornness as well, and she wasn't even a Forbes by birth—though some believed she might have been a distant cousin, connected through the Moynihan line way back. Si wouldn't let her go. Wouldn't get her a proper burial. Wouldn't leave her or let her be taken away. Well, turned out what was good for the goose was fine by the gander. Clarabelle's spirit left her body, but she never left the house. She hung around, haunted the old bugger, called him over. "Si," she said, "you've suffered enough."

"Not so much stubborn as kindhearted, Clarabelle was," Smith told Barbara. "She couldn't stand to leave the old bastard behind, so she took him with her."

After the funeral, when they were sure the other relatives had cleared out, Smith and Barbara slipped over to Dreams End, let themselves in with a key she'd finagled, dragged out Clarabelle's bed, mattress, bedding, book, and burned them in Si's meadow, along with some brush, cardboard boxes, and barn boards to perk up the fire. They burned the pillows, the sheets, and the log-cabin quilt in which Si had wrapped her.

All in all, it made for a good hot burn, smoky at times. At their height, the flames reached eight or ten feet and roared like something wild and frightened. It was a beautiful thing.

Another year, clover would mark the spot where the fire had been. From ash comes clover. Smith knows this because in winter he tosses ash from his wood stove over the snow between the cabin and the well house, and that's where the clover grows come spring.

The fire crackled and the smoke enveloped them. Smith and Barbara stepped back.

The veneer on the bedstead curled, the wood beneath blackened, charcoaled, glowed. Dusk settled. Then night. Then, in the shimmer of heat, Smith saw Boy, big as life, bigger even, and smiling. Or maybe Smith only imagined he was smiling, because he liked to think of Boy, Clarabelle, and Si reunited, getting along good.

He was pretty sure Barbara saw the ghost, too. Her face was flushed from the heat. Ash sprinkled the dark mass of her hair. The whites of her eyes turned pink from the smoke. She, too, stared at the place where Boy hovered somewhere between this world and the next, until the image faded into smoke and the smoke blew away.

Neither spoke of it. Barbara poked the coals with a long-handled hoe, raising sparks.

"Careful there." Smith brushed embers from his sleeve.

"What'd I do, set you on fire?"

"Not yet," he said.

After a while, the air changed, and the smoke rose straight up, as though drafted through an invisible chimney.

"Another weird thing," he said, because it felt like Boy had, just then, given him permission to say so: "The day Boy died, my mother took to her bed with a sick headache. The worst she ever had. And she never got up from that bed again. Or if she did, I never knew it. After that, I wouldn't step foot in the house, and she couldn't step out. You remember that, Barbara? You remember when Boy died?"

"I wasn't born," she said. "He died a month before I was born."

"You remember her, my mother. They called her Grammie Old, even in the village."

"Course I do," Barbara said. "She gave me chocolates. She had wonderful eyes."

"There's a lot of her in you. There's a lot of that woman in you, Barbara."

After a while, the fire settled into itself and began to die. Far away, they could hear the rush of the swollen river, anticipating ice.

*January 5, 1960*

### BOY

Sitting on the lightning bolt boulder, sucks the last of the medicine tea from the mug. "All tired out, huh," Smith says. "Spleeny. Can't keep up with the old man." He scrapes at the teeth of the crosscut with the file, metal on metal, almost music.

Through the tea steam, Boy's eyes are nearly as dark as the black in the red and black jacket balled up beside him. "Sure I can."

They compare strength. Boy squeezes Smith's muscle through his thick shirt. Smith squeezes Boy's. The muscles in Boy's arms are hard as his uncle's. "Ha," Smith says, "I could still trounce you, Boy—and I'm practically an old man."

"I'm taller," Boy says.

"I'd trounce you right now," Smith says, "if I wa'n't afraid it'd get me in Dutch with Clarabelle."

"Two hundred fifteen pounds," Boy says, "last count."

"Yeah, but soft, like all the other lazy young fellas."

"No, I'm not."

"Well, get to work then. What'll your father say, he gets back from the mill and that red oak still standing? What you sitting on your ass for wasting daylight?"

"All right," Boy says. "You too."

"All right."

Smith pulls one way on the crosscut. Boy pulls the other. Sharp-

ening has made the work easy. Back and forth, sluice and slice, the
blade singing toward the heart of the tree. And the tree singing, too.
And Boy and Smith keeping rhythm. Music. Lucretia kept her music in an alligator bag no one else was supposed to touch. But Boy
did. Once. He and his mother, father and Grammie Old were invited to Lucretia and Mim's house for boiled dinner because it was
harvest time and Lucretia was feeling better. In the spring, they'd
taken her off to County Hospital for treatment, but it seemed like
the treatment made her sicker not better. She threw up all day and
night, Mim said. She practically threw up her own guts. Another
secret: Boy overheard Lucretia say to Clarabelle maybe she should
just die and get it over with.

He didn't tell Mim.

Now, though, Lucretia felt well enough to cook, and eat, and
have company. "No thanks to those butchers down to County Hospital," his father said. "Grammie's medicine tea does more good
than anything they do to a body down to that God forsaken place."

"Eat your beets," Boy's mother said to Boy. "These beets are delicious, Lucretia. So sweet!"

"The ground was especially sweet this year," Lucretia said.

"A good year for root plants," Grammie said. "And root plants
are good for your heart." She was looking at Lucretia, but reached
across the table in Boy's direction, palm forward, fingers spread, as
though she would touch his heart. But he was too far away for her
reach, even when he leaned in, so he touched the place on his chest
where his own heart beat. "That's right," Grammie Old said. Her
eyes smiled.

Mim said: "Your heart's on the other side, Boy. A person's heart
is on the left."

"Some are," Grammie Old said.

"Where do you put your hand when you say the Pledge of Al-
legiance then?" Mim said.

Boy put his fingers to his forehead. A salute.

They all laughed, even Boy's father. Boy ducked his head, grinning, and forked a slice of corned beef toward his mouth, but it fell

apart midair. Some fell into his plate; some fell on the tablecloth where it made a greasy splotch that looked like a horse's head. He scooped the stringy meat in his napkin, but the splotch stayed.

Everything had been going along perfect—beets sweet, Lucretia feeling better, and all of them laughing, but now . . . He shifted his plate to cover the sin. It was such a pretty tablecloth, fancy lace, embroidered white on white with flowers and vines. Lucretia's best tablecloth.

Nobody noticed what he'd done at first, but they would. His father would be angry. His mother would be sorry. Mim would be glad she hadn't been the one. Lucretia would say: "No harm done," but it would be a kind lie. He felt so bad about the spot and so nervous wondering when it would be discovered, he couldn't eat. He pushed at the soft food on his plate with his fork, but the fork felt light as paper, hardly strong enough to pick anything up and convey it to his mouth, even if he wanted to. Which he didn't. Lucretia was pretending to eat, too. She'd raise a fork-full to her mouth, then lower it to the plate without so much as a nibble. She'd move her mouth like there was something in it. But there wasn't.

Food that had looked so good at first now looked poisonous— brown carrots, pink turnips, falling-apart onions. The beets looked like they were bleeding. Mim dissected a large one. Lucretia and his mother were listening to Grammie, in the middle of an old-days story about a pair of fine bay horses belonged to her brother Eff. His father sliced more corned beef. Mim mashed her beet into her potato, carrots, turnips. She drew shapes in the mash with the tip of her knife. Boy slipped low in his chair, then out of it, and quietly from the room. No one called after him. No one seemed to notice him slipping away and soon he was out of sight, moving through the piano room, into the big front hall—more like a cave than a room. He could hide here. They didn't notice he was gone for a long time.

They didn't look for him for a long time.

They didn't find him for a long time, either.

It was cool in the big front hall, and dark except for a small bulb high up. The walls were paneled wood. The floor was thin carpet. He crept into the perfumed tunnel of coats hanging one over another on the hall tree. Warm there and dark. He crept all the way to the wall, bumped his head on Lucretia's alligator bag, hanging from a special hook. The bag had a curved bone handle and heavy clasp. The leather was the lacquered hide of a real alligator that had once been alive in a swamp in a faraway place. He'd seen it before, but never up close. He had never seen a live alligator because there aren't any in New Hampshire. He'd like to see an alligator. From the look of Lucretia's bag, an alligator must be as beautiful as a garter snake. He rubbed the nubbly shine with respectful fingertips.

A long time later, when his mother tunneled in after him, she pried the bag from his hands. "That belongs to your Aunt Lucretia," she said. "It's personal. Now come back to the dinner table and be a good boy."

He'd just wanted to run his fingers over the nubbly skin and spring the clasp open and closed—snap!—like an alligator's jaw. But when he tried, the bag slipped from its special hook, fell open on the floor, and a few beautiful notes floated out like bells ringing—which was how he knew where Lucretia kept the music. His mother must have heard it too, and that was how she found him. "Put Aunt Lucretia's pocketbook back where you found it," his mother said. "Just as you found it."

He said he was sorry.

"I know," she said. "Just come back to dinner. Will you come with me now? There's gingerbread," and led him to the dining room, to the table, to his chair where all the eyes were looking at him. The gingerbread was shiny on top, golden brown inside. Lucretia cut square portions, lifted them with a spatula; slid them onto small plates. His father said: "You think a boy that sneaks off in the middle of dinner and we don't even know where he went and his mother gets all worked up and worried, you think that boy deserves gingerbread?"

Boy didn't answer. He didn't look at his father. He looked instead at the grease splotch where his plate used to be but somebody had taken it away.

"No harm done," Lucretia said.

"Si, pass your son his gingerbread," Grammie said.

Boy didn't want it. "Go ahead," Lucretia said. "Just a taste or my feelings will be hurt." He couldn't.

His mother said: "Now Si, look what you've done. Was that necessary?"

Boy's father said, "Go ahead, Boy. Eat. Lucretia made it special."

"Too sweet, I think," Lucretia said. "Too much molasses."

"Not too sweet," Boy's mother said.

Mim whispered to Boy, "Where'd you go?"

Lucretia said: "Tend to your own plate, Mim. Mind your business, now."

Grammie said, "You need cream on your gingerbread," and slid the bowl in his direction. Whipped cream grainy with sugar standing up in little peaks. He couldn't say thank you because his throat choked closed like he'd swallowed a sock. *Sorry sorry sorry*, he thought. *Sorry sorry . . .*

Uncle Smith speaks to him from far away. He sounds cross, but when Boy studies his face he doesn't look it. "Stay with me, Boy," Smith says from the other side of the world, the other end of the crosscut saw. "Just a little longer. I think we got this red oak bastard about licked." Smith pulls one way. Boy pulls the other. His arms ache. His head aches. A lay-down-in-the-dark headache coming on. Grammie has them, too. Sometimes the medicine tea staves them off. Sometimes it eases them. He wills the headache to go. Sometimes that works, too.

Whatever became of Lucretia's alligator bag? What became of her music? Did she take it with her when she died? Maybe the butchers at the County Hospital stole it. His father said before they got through with her, the bastards took everything she had, including the house. Which is why, after Lucretia died, Mim had to move away. He misses her.

Boy tips his head as though to drain the hurt of the memory. He feels the squeeze in his spine, the opening of his throat to the air, the winter sun speckling his eyes. Lucretia was sick for a long time and then she died. They buried her in the Pine Woods Cemetery.

When one of the Vermont cousins, a minister, was saying words over her grave, Boy looked across the rows and rows of gravestones to the part of the cemetery where nobody was buried yet. There, silhouetted against the cast-iron fence—just as the Vermont cousin said "The Lord is my shepherd," and the others joined in—Boy spotted a coyote: fine-furred and still, ears perked, gleaming.

Boy was standing between his father and Uncle Smith. He poked each of them in the side and pointed with his chin and eyes. They saw the coyote, too. His father said: "Would you look at that?" very soft because the prayer was still being prayed. Smith said, very soft, "Ain't that something?"

Smith calls out from far away, the other side of the world, the other end of the crosscut: "Where are you, Boy?"

"Right here." Boy pulls hard to prove it.

Smith releases his grip and steps back. "Time for a breather anyway. You think?"

Boy nods. The tree creaks and sways. Boy looks up. The sky is bright. He sees black branches against the flat blue of the sky. The tree splits. A limb high up has torn free, pulling half the trunk with it. Red heart wood, but black where it has died. And the whole business falling. He watches it fall—slow, slow—as though the tree is a mile high.

Or maybe the limb isn't falling but Boy is rising to meet it and everything else holding still.

Sky so blue; limb so dark. Too late to run which way?

"Move," Smith hollers. It's all he has time to say before the widow-maker crumples Boy like paper and he's pinned; the bulk of the limb heavy across his chest, its picks and branches scratching him all over, the earth hard under his back, a sticking-up rock pressing his tailbone, something poking his leg so sharp for a minute he thinks he must have fallen on his hunting knife.

"Jesus," Smith grunts. "Heavy goddamn son-of-a-bitch." He's try-ing to lift the limb. He's hugging it, pulling, the heels of his boots grinding the frozen ground. *My Uncle Smith is strong*, Boy thinks. He tries to help, too. Expands his chest. Pushes up with hands and stiff wrists.

"Friggin' red oak," Smith says. "Hollow in the middle. Sweet suf-fering Christ." But he's lifting it. An inch. Two inches. And Boy is rolling out from under.

He's rolling over the ground, clear.

"Jesus," Smith says. "Why the hell di'n't you jump when I told you?"

"I'm all right." Boy tries to stand but can't find his legs, finds his knees and elbows instead. Smith hoists him by the shoulders.

"Course you're all right," Smith says. "Got a little bung on your head, that's all. Got a little scraped up, that's all. No broken arm, no broken leg, no broken back, no broken neck. Hey, you're doing all right for a fella got flattened by a Christly red oak."

Boy presses the heel of his hand to his temple. When he takes his hand away, it is wet with blood. Blood in his eye, too. He's seeing out of one eye, because blood sheets the other. Smith mops at him with his handkerchief. "Jesus," he says. "You're bleeding."

"Jesus," Boy says. "I guess I am."

*August 24, 1991*

### SMITH

Grumbles into the collar of his flannel shirt. The neck is three sizes too big, and when he tucks his head he's talking into the top button as though it were a microphone. "Seventy dollars?" he says. "For that thing? Sweet suffering Christ."

### AND-FIVE-WHERE?

He raises his chin, stubbled with white needles poking out through the skin. Shakes his head: "Am I the only goddamn Forbes left with any goddamn sense? What are they after, Barbara, that beat-up old box thing?"

"They're bidding off Grammie Old's sewing cabinet," Barbara says, hair pulled away from her face and spiraling out from under the bright band, eyes snappy as beans.

"It's the aunts," she says, "Poppy and Mim in a bidding war."

Smith doesn't have to look at the cabinet to know exactly what it is: hand-planed pine, slide-away top with three drawers below and bins on either side. Tongue-and-groove. Stands about three feet high on turned legs. Set right there in the parlor all his life, between the horse-hair settee and the Morris chair. "Come down to my mother from her mother and the Moynihans. Rode over on the boat from the old country probably; stuffed full of seed potatoes, probably. Set right there in the parlor, Barbara, for a hundred years and nobody thought anything of it. Jesus H. Christ—seventy dollars! I could eat for two months on seventy dollars."

"That's why you're so skinny," she says. "That's why we worry about you blowing away in a brisk wind. You get much skinnier, we'll have to peg you down at the corners like George's tent."

He's perched himself on the domed lid of the trunk she paid ten dollars for a few minutes ago. About nine dollars more than it's worth. Smith wouldn't give two cents for it, himself. The hinges are rusted, ready to snap; the leather handles worn to stubs. He knocks a knuckle against the wooden slatting. Punky. He knocks the pressed tin on the side. Don't sound empty. Knocks again. Don't sound full. The trunk is latched and locked. No key, of course. COULD BE TREASURES IN THERE, George had said. WHO KNOWS?

"Treasures my ass," Smith says.

"My treasure." Barbara holds a quilt out to him—nonsense colors and all different shapes—must be a thousand pieces, and no two the same. A lot more to it than that old, brown, stained thing they burned together in the meadow last fall.

"I bid it off and now it's mine. I was thinking of giving it to my mother. Making my father pay for it and then giving it to her just to irritate Grenadine. But I don't know if I can part with it."

"My mother made that quilt," he says. "I believe so. I've got a vague recollection." Seems like a memory, maybe a dream: her in the Morris chair evenings, the lamp tilted to light up the piecework in her lap. Sewing cabinet open, cloth spilling from the bin, spools on rods. The in and out of the needle. Flash of thimbles, one on either hand.

And this went on for years. The year or two or three after his father went through the ice. The house was quiet then, especially evenings, and she'd sit for hours, stitching, humming sometimes so low you could hardly hear her. The rest of them would go off to bed, heavy-eyed—he and Si, Lucretia, Hamilton—but she'd stay up late, stitching. "That quilt'll keep you warm in a cold snap, Barbara, but what the hell you want with some old trunk, you don't even know what's in it?"

"That's why," she says. "For the surprise. And besides, you needed a place to sit." She folds the quilt, places it beside him on the trunk like a pillow. "Keep your eye on Grammie's quilt," she says. "Don't let anyone touch it, especially not Grenadine."

AND-NOW-THE-NINETY, George says. ARE YOU ALL DONE AT A HUNDRED? AND-FIVE-AND-TEN-AND-FIFTEEN WHERE?

"A hundred dollars," he says. "A hundred dollars? I'm going home."

"No you're not. You sit right there. Move over."

He shifts to make room, lifts himself up and settles again. As he moves, his hand presses an indentation on the center slat. The wood has darkened and the carving is shallow, but he can make it out, by touch if not by sight. He traces the lines with a finger. Just the three block letters, rough hewn: B-O-Y.


*January 5, 1960*

### NEXT THING

Boy knows he's in the cab of a moving pickup. Head hurts. Shoulder hurts. Back stiff as a pole. Can't move because he's wedged between two big men and it's a tight fit.

Boy doesn't recognize the driver—dark skinned, scoop nosed, hair clipped so short you can't tell the color. Sunset glares off the lenses of his glasses. Smith leans in: "Welcome to the land of the living."

"I went away," Boy says. "But now I'm back."

"It was a bitch getting you out of the woods. Just about all I could do to drag your sorry carcass out after you fell down on me. 'Bout like dragging a two hundred pound deer uphill through the pucker brush."

"Two hundred fifteen," Boy says, "last count."

"You wa'n't no help at all, Boy. Had to recruit this fella here once I got you to the road; had to commandeer the vehicle."

"How you feeling?" the driver says. His magnified eyes seem alien. His ears are big and sticking out, angel wings.

"A tree fell on my head."

"He's tough," Smith says. "We'll just get him checked out. Take a stitch or ten. Get some pretty nurse to give him a shot in the ass. You'll be all set then, Boy."

"I'm all right."

"You been bleeding all over this fella's truck. That's not too good. Goddammit, you must be down a quart. Or two."

Boy thinks the driver might be mad because of the blood. "Sorry," he says.

"I'd stitch you up myself," Smith says, "but, dammit, left my needle and thread to home. Here now, peel your hand off your head. Let's have a look at that ding."

Next thing, it's night and the truck bumps to a stop in front of a square building lit up, a hundred windows like a hundred yellow eyes. Boy hunkers down in the cab. People moving in those eyes. A lot of them.

Smith and the driver try to maneuver him out of the truck, but he braces his hands on the door frame. Feet, too. "Can you stand up?" the driver says. "Feeling wobbly, son?"

Smith says, "Grab hold of me, and we'll hoof it right on through to 'mergency."

"I'm not going in there," Boy says. "I'm not."

Smith shakes his head. "Forbes-stubborn," he says. "No need of it."

Smith and the stranger step away into a circle of light from the pole lamp, tall as a tree, with a bulb so bright it hums. They talk at each other. Boy doesn't even try to make out what they're saying. He doesn't want to hear another word about 'mergency. *Going home*, he thinks. *Going home. Going home.* After a while, Smith calls over to him, "Don't run off now," and strides toward the building. The big glass doors swish open and suck him in. The driver studies Boy's face. "Sit tight." He steps in front of the truck, rests his long back against the curve of the hood, lights a cigarette in cupped hands. Through the cloudy windshield, the cigarette glows bright, then fades, brightens again.

Boy slides from the truck like butter melting. Tests his legs, expecting them to melt too, but they are stiff as stilts hinged on his hips. They hold his weight. They work fine, and he's stiff-walking into the night, the pavement spongy under his soles. The driver, smoking, notices nothing. Boy melts into the darkness at the edge of the parking lot. No one sees. He's across the yellow-lined road, wading through cat-o-nine-tails, pushing through leafless bushes higher than his head. Hears a siren not far away, drawing closer.

*They can't get me in the woods*, he thinks. Safe among trees. He can see like a cat, moves easily along a path he senses or creates. Follows his shadow. Sometimes he stumbles. Sometimes he runs. Mostly he walks until he can't hear traffic anymore. Can't hear sirens. Can't hear anything but the harsh in and out of his breath and the drum of his heart.

Later, another sound: water flowing under a skim of ice. He follows the brook just as Smith and his father said to if he ever got lost. He never got lost before. He's not lost now. He follows the brook, which opens into a body of water, an expanse of ice, silvery in moonlight. Tree shadows. Bush shadows. Rock shadows. Boy shadow. Boy and his shadow step onto the ice. It holds their weight like magic.

This is not a lake, he decides, or even a pond. It's a swamp, not too deep. Swamp grasses, paled by night, stick up through the ice. They whisper when he passes. *Home,* they say. *This way home.* Beyond the grasses, the ice smooth for gliding. He glides one foot forward, then the other, swings his arms for momentum. He is skating on his boots. He is falling and rolling. He is laughing. Farther out, sentinel trees, long dead from flooding and peeled to dry-ki, cast armed shadows. He skates among them, embraced, making good time. The wind of his motion is music. He spins. Falls on his butt. Laughs. Sits up. Hugs his knees. Ahead the white ice darkens. The shoreline beyond is familiar. *Home.*

He is not far from home. He recognizes the elephant rock, the leaning birch. The landing. The shoulder of Forbes Mountain rising behind. Small Pond. He knows the way from here! He knows every stone and hummock, every turn of the old wood road. Pretty soon he'll be trudging along that road. Pretty soon he'll crest the hill, turn the corner, and there's his house. The lights will be on in the kitchen; his father and mother at the table. They'll say: "Where you been?"

He'll say: "I went away. But now I'm back."

Ahead, where the ice darkens, something is moving, a familiar, four-legged shadow racing toward him. Chip-dog.

"Chip-dog," he calls. "Where you been?"

The dog, startled, goes into a skid.

"Slippery," Boy says.

Chip-dog, spread-eagled.

"It's me," Boy says.

Then the tail starts to wag, then the dog's whole behind. "I'm coming." Boy pumps his arms to help his legs move faster. He's sliding, skating, flying; he's shooshing through a sheet of water that makes the ice even slicker. Greasy. Couldn't stop now if he wanted to. Doesn't want to. He's laughing, singing. "You wait right there, Chip-dog," he calls. "You wait right there."

*January 5, 1960*

## CLARABELLE

Waited at home with Grammie Old, sick in bed and shouldn't be left alone. Clarabelle wanted to go out searching with the others; she wanted to ride and walk and call his name; but she had to content herself with keeping Grammie company.

"He'll be heading home," Si had said, "where he should have been brought in the first place. Where any half-wit would have known, should have known, to bring him in the first place."

"He was bleeding from the head," Smith said. "A goddamn tree fell on him."

"Yuh, and why was that?" Si said. "Whose fault was that, huh?"

"A goddamn tree fell on him," Smith said.

"Stupid son-of-a-bitch, dragging that poor hurt boy the last place he could stand to be. Scared to death—and why wouldn't he be after the job those butchers did on him getting him born? Course he run. Course he did."

"Stop it," Clarabelle said.

But how could they?

How would he ever find his way back, she wondered. So dark. So cold. So far. Then she remembered last night's dream of swallows and how Grammie Old admitted, over breakfast, she dreamed the same.

*August 24, 1991*

## MIM

Wants to say to Poppy: "Why do you have to be so stubborn?"

Course she doesn't.

AND NOW THE TWENTY, George suggests. ONE-HUNDRED-AND-TWENTY.

"Yes," Poppy says.

"Five," Mim says.

AND-THIRTY?

Poppy nods. Forbes-stubborn and been that way since she was a pouty golden-haired girl: plant your heels, cross your arms, set your jaw. No moving a Forbes then. Might just as well try to tip Forbes Mountain over with a spoon.

What does Poppy want with Grammie Old's sewing cabinet anyway? It's not like she sews or ever did. She'd throw her new husband's favorite argyle socks away sooner than darn a hole the size of a penny. Probably doesn't even own a darning needle. Nor thread.

Henry holds up the wooden darning egg, Boy's egg "Buddy," pulled from the right-hand bin. He raises the egg over his head, cupped—almost tenderly, almost as though it were a real egg—in his palm.

Poppy wouldn't know what to do with that egg if she had it. Wouldn't know enough to stuff it into the toe of her new husband's favorite argyle sock to stretch the hole for darning. Poppy might *need* that egg, those buttons, that thread, the silks and velvets, the dear old pin cushion—but she wouldn't *use* them. She'd display them like her commemorative plates.

WHAT ELSE YOU FINDING, HENRY? George says. THAT CABINET CHOCK FULL OF TREASURES, AIN'T IT.

Henry holds up his other hand, a thimble on the tip of each finger. "Chock full," he says. "Bursting at the seams." He twiddles his fingers and the thimbles catch the light. "The contents may be worth more'n the cabinet, wouldn't surprise me." He has thin hands that strike Mim as dainty for a man, strong but thin and well formed, graceful in their own way as roadside lilies.

She falls in love, "One fifty!" and presses her bidding card to her chest, hard as if a whoosh of wind might tug the card away and there she'd be without a number. Poppy would surely take advantage. With her other hand she's squeezing Evangeline's middle. "Ouch ouch ouch," Evangeline says. "My organs would be squished if I had any. Mim, ouch, you're popping my seams." A pin in the waistband of Evangeline's apron penetrates the flesh at the base of Mim's thumb.

"Ouch," Mim says, sucking the wound.

"Don't bleed on me," Evangeline says.

Mim bleeds into a ball of tissue.

Henry drops the thimbles one by one into the right-hand bin. They fall in slow motion, like tiny silver parachutes, landing softly— maybe the bin is full of fabric after all. Or yarn. Or cotton batting. Or a muslin doll.

"Like me!" Evangeline says.

Or a nightgown Grammie Old never got around to mending. Mim would mend it. And wear it. Soft old cotton, like memories of loved ones comforting you as you sleep. And farther down in the bin: Great Aunt Rosa's hatpin with the amber stone, flat as a sunflower hull, smooth as an eye. Lace and pearl from Great Aunt Molly's gossamer gown. A velvet drawstring bag of scrap ribbon. Tatting half-tatted on the spool.

George says: ARE WE ALL DONE AT ONE-HUNDRED-FIFTY DOLLARS?

Henry's nostrils flare. A drop of something (sweat? mucus?) takes shape at the end of his nose. He pulls a rumpled handkerchief from his back pocket, wipes his nose, blows like an elk.

Mim falls out of love.

"Who made that last bid?" Lucy says. "I've lost track."

Her husband, just back from the lunch wagon with a cardboard tray of hot dogs, sets it on Lucy's lap and snakes the baby into his arms, lifts him high, jiggles him to laughter. The baby reaches for his daddy's beard, latches on, now he's doing baby pull-ups.

Jim says, "I think the bid is on that guy behind you. He's been bidding right along."

"The one fifty's on me," Mim says.

"No, I believe the bid is mine." It's the pewter-haired dealer who smells like the sea. "You were bidding with such enthusiasm, de-ahs," he says to Mim and Poppy. "It's contagious."

Mim wants to stick him deep and in a tender spot with Great Aunt Rosa's amber hatpin. Poppy wants to grab him by a shag of pewter hair and pull. Jim wants to know what aftershave he uses.

GOING-ONCE GOING-TWICE . . .

Mim raises her card, flutters it like a flag. "Here," she shouts, "right here."

*I want you to have it, Mim.* It is as if Grammie Old spoke—just then—directly in her ear. Mim looks: nobody there. A shiver passes over her, head to toe; her cheek and the soft underside of her jaw cooled by a tickle of ghostly breath. Not breath exactly—ghosts don't breathe, do they?—more the essence of an invisible someone close by and adamant.

George squints in Mim's direction. She holds her breath. Grammie Old speaks again—stern this time, plain as the skip of Mim's heart, clear as a pewter bell: *You Mim. I want you to have it.*


*Late 1960s*

### SI

And Clarabelle weren't famous for their housekeeping. Hard to keep a house spicky-spandy when it's full of this and that, old and older, outdated, obsolete, old-fashioned (can't even recall what it was used for originally), but too good to throw away, might come in handy some day, and doesn't even belong to you really, belongs to the family, passed down through the generations and you are only the caretaker.

If you could walk through a room unimpeded, good enough.

Clarabelle didn't give a hoot if the toys in the toy-room were scattered wall to wall—old toys from other generations: carved animals and the ark, tin roly-polies, a wicker carriage full of soft dolls, some with celluloid heads and eyes that blinked, a crate of blocks. Sara would say: "You pick up, Barbara, before we go. Pick up, okay? All the ones you played with, you put them back where they belong."

Her father, Ham, would have his coat on and buttoned already—ready to go. Wherever they were and whatever amount of time they spent, he was always impatient to move on. Getting twitchy, Sara called it: "Your father's getting twitchy, Barbara. Hurry up. Put those things back where you found them."

But Clarabelle would intervene: "Leave the toys for next time.

Leave them just as they are. The little girl's got them all arranged, Sara, can't you see?" This followed by Sara's sigh of acquiescence—a mother's sigh that, to this day, sends shudders of guilt down Barbara's spine, even when she has nothing to be guilty about. When her child is born—a daughter, she feels it—Barbara will never sigh that way in her presence. In fact, she may give up sighing altogether.

And sure enough, the next time they visited Si and Clarabelle—unless that brat Lucy had come and gone—the toys would be just where Barbara had left them, along with dust kitties that blew like tumbleweeds when she opened the door. Sometimes when she was alone in the room, the dust kitties seemed to move on their own. She named the big ones, and imagined that they really were kitties, ghost kitties.

"Jackknife did the trick, Barbara. Look here." Smith has picked the lock on Boy's trunk. "It wa'n't hard," he says. "Scraped off the grit, poked at it a little. Pretty soon—bing! Snapped her right open."

"What's in there? Not a dead rat, I hope. I'll be very disappointed if it's a dead rat," Barbara says.

"What do you think I am, nosy as Houstiff?" Smith said. "I ain't looked. You bought it. You look."

They lift the lid together. Musty. A pervading mustiness. Barbara sneezes, pulls out a baby blanket, faded to gray, and folded for so long the lines seem permanent. Toddler shoes tied by their strings. Pint-sized overalls, patched in the knees and rear. A green felt fisherman's cap. An alligator skin pocketbook.

"What the hell." Smith said. "Lucretia brought that thing back from Florida. One trip down south when she was a young woman, didn't stay long, come back with this thing and . . . well, 'nough said on that subject." But Barbara knows it is the forbidden subject of Aunt Mim's conception and birth. She knows, they all know, straight-laced Lucretia had one child but never a husband.

Barbara snaps the purse open, reaches through tissue paper, and pulls out a key-wind, the size of a matchbox. She turns the key, and releases the strained notes of a song she doesn't recognize.

"Oh my God," Mim says. "I haven't seen that pocketbook in, I don't know, about a hundred years. Mother never used it. She kept it. One of her treasures. I thought it was long gone."

"You take it, Mim," Barbara says.

Mim hesitates. Barbara puts the pocketbook in Mim's hands. Mim sees that Barbara truly wants her to have it, and Grammie Old impressed on all of them what an insult it was to refuse the gift of a gift, even if the gift were one of those nasty chocolate drops from the jar.

"We'll trade," Mim says, and hands over Evangeline, finished now, from her rag-haired head to the lacy hem of her skirt. Evangeline doesn't protest.

"Mim," Barbara says. "There's no need."

Mim says, "Don't you dare refuse the gift of a gift."

Smith has lifted a sheaf of papers bound with string from a falling-apart box at the bottom of the trunk. He cuts off the string and the three of them—he, Barbara, Mim—paw through. Drawings on construction paper, from baby scribbles to sketches of the house, familiar faces, the rowboat, the river, a black tree against a clear sky.

"Boy was quite an artist," Mim says. "People didn't realize."

"He could do a lot of things people didn't realize," Smith says.

Among the drawings, Boy's birth certificate—with his real name and date of birth, mother's name Clarabelle Stewart Forbes; father, Si Moynihan Forbes. "It's my middle name, too. Smith says. "And my mother's name. And my brother's. Family name carried through."

Barbara found the death certificate too, black bordered parchment, with a Notary Public stamp and all things official. January 5, 1960, the certificate read. Death by drowning. Accidental.

"He was just trying to get home," Smith says.

"He was a sweet soul," Mim says. "The sweetest soul I ever knew."

In a corner, one more thing, the last thing, wrapped in newspaper, Barbara finds a bone-colored mug, heavy, dark with use inside. She runs her finger around the rim, gently—the way you'd touch a lover's mouth or the crown of a newborn's head. The chip is so worn it is no longer a flaw, more like sculpture.

If Brad came across this mug in the cupboard or dish drainer, he'd hold it out to her with the tips of his long artist's fingers, like a small corpse. "Barbara," he'd say, "We've been invaded!"

"I collected it from the woods the day after he died," Smith says. "Gave it to Clarabelle. Si told me to get the hell out and never come back, and by God, I never did—not until the time came last fall that I had to."

"I'm going to use it," Barbara says.

"I should think you would," Mim says. "It's a nice heavy mug. You could drop it on a stone floor and it wouldn't even break. These old ones keep your coffee warm for a long time. They're real handy."

Barbara tests the mug's weight, raises it toward her mouth, pretending to drink: a substantial mug, age-crackled and cracked but not all the way through. It is old and it is beautiful. Years of use have created a patina, like an exquisite web of wrinkles over a dear old face. ❧

## ABOUT THE AUTHOR

REBECCA RULE, a New Hampshire native, has published two other collections of short stories. *The Best Revenge* was named Outstanding Work of Fiction by the New Hampshire Writers Project and listed as one of five "Essential New Hampshire Books" by *New Hampshire Magazine*. She also co-authored two how-to books with Susan Wheeler: *Creating the Story* and *True Stories*. Since 1992, she's written a column on New Hampshire books and writers, "Bookmarks," which appears in the *Concord Monitor, Nashua Telegraph*, and *Portsmouth Herald*. To date, that adds up to over 500 columns.

Best known for her live presentations of humorous New Hampshire stories, many sponsored by the New Hampshire Humanities Council, she has entertained audiences from Stratford to Keene, prompting *New Hampshire Magazine* to name her "Thalia: the Muse of Comedy" in its list of notable New Hampshire muses. Her CDs are "Perley Gets a Dump Sticker," and "Better Than a Poke in the Eye." She often performs with other writers, including poets Diana Durham, Neil English, and Claire Robson. A roster artist for the New Hampshire State Council on the Arts, her passion for the spoken word sometimes takes her to schools, helping young writers find their voices. And for more than ten years she has served on the steering committee for the New Hampshire Young Writers Conference.

She also co-hosts, with Maren Tirabassi, a monthly radio program, "Speaking Volumes: A Literary Variety Show," on WSCA 106.1 Portsmouth Community Radio. For Friends of the UNH Libraries she hosts the interview show "The Authors Series," which airs occasionally on NHPTV.

OTHER BOOKS BY REBECCA RULE

WOOD HEAT: STORIES FROM UP NORTH

THE BEST REVENGE: SHORT STORIES

CREATING THE STORY: GUIDES FOR WRITERS
(WITH SUSAN WHEELER)

TRUE STORIES: GUIDES FOR WRITING FROM YOUR LIFE
(WITH SUSAN WHEELER)